In the Shadow of Aldersgate

In the Shadow of Aldersgate

*An Introduction to the Heritage
and Faith of the Wesleyan Tradition*

Daniel L. Burnett

CASCADE *Books* · Eugene, Oregon

IN THE SHADOW OF ALDERSGATE
An Introduction to the Heritage and Faith of the Wesleyan Tradition

Cascade Books
A Division of Wipf and Stock Publishers
199 West 8th Avenue, Suite 3
Eugene, Oregon 97401

ISBN: 978-1-59752-573-2

Cataloging-in-Publication Data:

Burnett, Daniel L.

  In the shadow of Aldersgate : an introduction to the heritage and faith of the Wesleyan tradition / Daniel L. Burnett.

        viii + 183 p.; 23 cm.

Includes bibliographical references.

ISBN 1-59752-573-1 (alk. paper)

1. Wesley, John, 1703–1791. 2. Methodism—History. 4. Methodism—Doctrines. I. Title.

BX8331 B86 2006

Manufactured in the U.S.A.

Contents

Part 2

The Wesleyan Passion:
A Dynamic Meeting of Grace and Faith / 67

Part 3

The Wesleyan Vision:
Practical Holiness in the Real World / 137

Abbreviations

Introduction

"A Settled Resolution"

IN 1784 the eighty-one year old John Wesley still possessed a sharp mind and clear memory. While writing a sermon entitled "In What Sense We Are to Leave the World," he thought back to his student days at Oxford University some sixty years earlier. He included in the sermon his recollection of a determined decision he had made in Oxford at about the age of twenty-two. That, he said, was "When it pleased God to give *me* a settled resolution to be not a *nominal* Christian but a *real* Christian."[1]

Though raised from birth in a rigorous Christian environment by highly devout parents, the young Wesley had never understood that the true goal of religion is inward holiness rather than outward duty. Finally, at the age of twenty-two he came to realize that real Christianity is clearly distinct from outward or nominal Christianity. He was intimately familiar with the liturgical forms and ecclesiastical structures of Christianity in eighteenth century England, but now he was awakened to the possibility of something more. He wanted to be intimately familiar with the Christ of Christianity.

That commitment to real Christianity became the driving force of Wesley's life and the movement that exploded under his leadership. It was the passion that took him down many roads of spiritual pursuit and ministry activity—a disciplined life, missionary service in America, pilgrimage to Moravia, extensive itinerate preaching, economic relief for the poor, education for the illiterate, training of preachers, writing and publishing.

By his own admission, however, the early years of strict discipline and determined action failed to achieve the goal of his "settled resolution." Sincere as his efforts were, they were just that—*his* efforts. It would be several years before he would experience and understand the transforming power of God's saving and sanctifying grace. Once he did, he was never again the same.

---

[1] *Works* 6:473.

John Wesley did not invent a new theology. As a loyal Englishman and minister in the Church of England he held rigorously to the doctrine of his Anglican heritage. Through the course of his spiritual and intellectual development, however, he came to embrace certain beliefs that had gone out of fashion in much of the church and culture of his time. Most notable were the ideas that (1) God offers saving grace freely to all, (2) God enables all to either accept or reject that grace, and (3) God provides sanctifying power to all believers that they might experience holiness of heart and life. In short, John Wesley simply encountered the full impact of what he saw in the biblical message of Good News. He discovered that through God's grace and power it truly is possible to be a real Christian in the real world.

What at the age of twenty-two was a well-intended determination, at the age of thirty-five became a radical meeting with divine grace. In the years following his famous Aldersgate Street conversion, human effort gave way to divine control. Disciplined duty found fulfillment in divine love. Fearful doubts discovered assurance in divine presence. The power of sin was overcome by the power of grace.

The result? John Wesley was a changed man, thousands more were transformed by the gospel he preached, and millions since have come to share in his "settled resolution to be not a *nominal* Christian but a *real* Christian." These are the people who walk in the shadow of Aldersgate.

Part 1

The Wesleyan Story:
*John Wesley's Quest for Authentic
Christianity*

1

Piety and Good Intentions

Wesley's England

A Christian Birthright

CHRISTIANITY WAS certainly nothing new to England by Wesley's time. According to early legends the faith was in the British Isles within decades of Jesus' life. Some legends say the gospel was first preached in England by Joseph of Arimathea and in Scotland by the apostle Andrew. While there is no historical evidence to support these claims, it is known that Christians were an established minority on the island by the beginning of the third century. Britain was under Roman military occupation from 55 BC to AD 409. British Christianity most likely owes its origins to that occupation and the unnamed Roman soldiers and officials who brought their Christian faith to the region.

AD 597 is the year cited as the official beginning of Christianity in Britain. That was when Pope Gregory commissioned St. Augustine for a mission to evangelize the English. (This Augustine should not be confused with the famous theologian, St. Augustine of Hippo, who died in AD 430.) Augustine's mission met with great success, primarily through the conversion of Ethelbert, king of Kent. The church was established at Canterbury and Augustine became the first Archbishop of Canterbury. In reality, the faith had already been active for several centuries. The earlier presence had spread among the native Celtic people of Britain and developed its own tradition of doctrine, worship, and mission. The most famous of the Celtic Christians were St. Patrick, who took the faith from England to Ireland in the fifth century; and St. Columba, who left Ireland a century later to evangelize Scotland and northern England. But within a hundred years of Augustine's arrival in England, Roman Christianity had grown to a position of dominance over Celtic Christianity. Celtic Christianity continued to function in the British Isles, but British Christianity on the whole came under the control of Rome.

Things changed dramatically during the reign of Henry VIII (1509–47). After some twenty years of marriage to Catherine of Aragon, Henry had no male heir. Concerned about the instability this could cause in the event of his death, he sought to obtain a divorce so he could marry his mistress, Anne Boleyn, and produce a male heir. Due to the interconnected system of church power and state politics, such a drastic move required the sanction of Pope Clement VII. For political reasons of his own, Clement denied Henry's request. Henry eventually resolved the problem by declaring himself, and therefore his entire country, to be no longer under the authority of the Roman Church. Instead, England would now have its own national church with Henry as its head. Thus, the obstacle to Henry's divorce was removed and the protestant Church of England was born.

It is from this backdrop that the Christianity of Wesley's day developed. In the eighteenth century English Christianity was divided into three main categories: Anglican (Church of England), Roman Catholic, and Dissenters. The Dissenters were also known as Nonconformists. They included various protestant churches that remained outside the Church of England. Quakers, Baptists, Presbyterians, Congregationalists, and independents were all dissenting churches. Most people identified with one of these three church categories, though few ever attended worship services.

The Christianity of Wesley's England was in a state of serious decline. Pastors were paid "livings" from government tax revenues to oversee their appointed parishes. Many of these pastors, however, rarely if ever visited the churches under their care. Instead, they paid meager salaries to curates (assistants), who were often poorly equipped, to serve in their absence while they lived off their government subsidies in London or other distant locations. It is reported that in 1750, barely one half of the official parishes were ever entered by the clergymen who were being paid to care for them.[1]

Simply stated, British Christianity was suffering from a nearly fatal infestation of nominalism. Church structure, hierarchy, and conformity were paramount. Spiritual vitality was almost nonexistent. In fact, it was openly discouraged and suppressed. Experiences and expressions of new birth and overt devotion were considered out of order. "Enthusiasm" was the derogatory label pinned on such spirituality. Those who indulged in these experiences were labeled as dangerous extremists who threatened to undermine the very structure of England society.

---

[1]   D. Michael Henderson, *John Wesley's Class Meeting: A Model for Making Disciples* (Nappanee, Ind.: Evangel, 1997) 20.

A Changing Society

John Wesley's life (1703–91) spanned almost the entire eighteenth century. It was the era famously described by Charles Dickens in *A Tale of Two Cities* as the best of times and the worst of times. It was a period that witnessed many changes within England's social environment. At the beginning of his life the vast majority of Britain's population lived in rural and village settings. By the end of his life the Industrial Revolution had drawn tens of thousands into rapidly growing urban centers. However, the new advances in technology did not result in corresponding advances in society. Thousands of men, women, and children were virtually enslaved by horrendous work conditions and long hours in the new industrial factories. Children as young as four years of age were routinely put to work in coal mines, factories, brickyards, and textile mills. Very few received any type of education. Poverty, disease, illiteracy, alcoholism, crime, poor housing, and substandard sanitation plagued the country. London, by far the largest city, was particularly notorious.

Lack of concern for the poor was attributed in part to the popular belief that the poor were fulfilling the predetermined destiny God had chosen for them. In other words, if God had wanted the poor to have better lives, he would have had them born into better families. Some even attempted to promote the idea that the poor were actually better off than the rich since they did not carry the burdens and responsibilities of wealth. However, the fact that people could and did rise and fall through the different layers of social and economic status demonstrates that social standing was not necessarily a permanent fixture.

It should also be noted that the eighteenth century did see many positive developments, although it was naturally those of high society who enjoyed the greatest benefit. Vast improvements in transportation were realized through a rapidly growing network of roads and canals. Scientific discoveries and understandings were expanding. Music, art, and culture flourished. The first foreign missionary societies were established. And the movement toward the abolition of slavery was underway.

All of these factors had at least some degree of impact on Wesley as a person and as a minister. The unique role that he played in the history of Britain and the history of the Christian church did not happen in a vacuum. He was a man of his own time and culture.

A Product of His Time

Questions from the Start

John Wesley was born in the small town of Epworth, England, to Samuel and Susanna Wesley. He seems to have been destined for a life of controversy from the very day he was born. Something as simple as the date of his birth has to be explained in order to decide which of two dates to use. He was born on June 17, 1703, but in 1752 England switched from the old style Julian calendar to the more accurate Gregorian calendar. When Wesley's birthday was adjusted to correspond with the modern calendar, June 28 became his new date of birth.

Surprisingly, there is also dispute over his name. He always gave his name as simply John Wesley. However, according to one longstanding tradition, his full name was actually John Benjamin Wesley. Even modern writers have arrived at different conclusions as to whether or not he had a middle name. Roy Hattersley states that he was christened John Benjamin, supposedly in memory of two earlier Wesley sons who died in infancy.[2] Wesley scholar Henry Rack dismisses this as a mistaken legend that originated early in the nineteenth century.[3] Neither Wesley nor his parents ever used or made reference to any middle name. Most authorities agree with Rack that his full name was simply John Wesley.

Influential Parents

Samuel was a Church of England priest who had been educated at the University of Oxford through Exeter College. His father and grandfather were also ministers, but in the Dissenters tradition. As a young man Samuel had decided to abandon his nonconformist roots and to dedicate himself to the doctrine and ministry of the Church of England. In 1688 he married Susanna Annesley at Marylebone Church in London. Over the next eight years he served three different parishes in addition to a short stint as a naval chaplain. He assumed the pastorate of St. Andrew's Church, Epworth in 1696 and remained there until his death in 1735.

In some ways Samuel was better suited to academic and literary pursuits than to pastoral ministry. He was an accomplished scholar, poet, and author who longed to make his mark on the literary world—a dream that remained

---

[2] Roy Hattersley, *A Brand from the Burning: The Life of John Wesley* (London: Little Brown, 2002) 20.

[3] Henry D. Rack, *Reasonable Enthusiast: John Wesley and the Rise of Methodism* (London: Epworth, 1992) 48.

unfulfilled. Nevertheless, Samuel was clearly a dedicated and conscientious pastor. However, he seemed to think of himself as a man of culture who really belonged with people of high society rather than the illiterate parishioners of a remote rural setting. These feelings were not without some degree of foundation, as the Wesley family did in fact have friendly connections among England's aristocracy and nobility. This may have been one of the reasons why he was often an unpopular figure in his community. There were also other reasons; for example, his sometimes overzealous efforts to discipline his parishioners and reform their conduct. There was also the matter of his politics. Samuel was a loyal supporter of the king, but the people of Epworth did not share his enthusiasm for the monarchy.

While no one questions Samuel's Christian integrity, most of his problems seemed to stem from his lapses of good judgment and common sense. This is seen most clearly in his inability to manage his finances. Although his salary should have been adequate, even for a family as large as his, the Wesleys lived in poverty. At one point he even served a prison term of several months because of his inability to repay a debt.

Samuel died three years before the beginning of the great revival movement that would make his two youngest sons, John and Charles, world famous. He was buried in the yard of St. Andrew's Church, Epworth.

Susanna Wesley was also the child of Dissenter parents. Her father, Dr. Samuel Annesley, was one of the best known and respected nonconformist ministers of his generation. He was an Oxford educated man who placed great value on the pursuit of learning. Although women had no access to higher education, the Annesley's saw that Susanna was properly educated. The Annesley home was always a placed filled with scholarly books, distinguished guests, and stimulating conversation. This rich environment instilled a passion and pattern for learning that was transferred through Susanna to her own children years later.

Susanna was the youngest of Dr. Annesley's twenty-five children (by two marriages). She demonstrated at an early age both a sharp aptitude for theological understanding and a strong spirit of independence. When just twelve years old she decided that she would leave the Dissenting church and join the Church of England, just as her future husband Samuel had done. She continued to utilize her independent spirit and sharp intellect throughout her life. Although always a devoted wife and mother, she did not shy away from standing her own ground with her husband and exercising firm authority over her children.

Susanna also showed that she possessed a compassionate pastoral quality along with strong leadership skills. When Samuel was away in London on extended church business in 1712, she became so dissatisfied with the poor quality of preaching being provided by Samuel's curate that she began leading Sunday afternoon meetings in the kitchen of the Epworth parsonage. Women were not allowed to preach, but she saw no reason why she could not read published sermons to her children and any others who wished to attend. Susanna's kitchen meetings became so popular that she claimed as many as 200 people sometimes arrived at their home. The jealous curate wrote to Samuel in London complaining that his wife was holding illegal meetings. Samuel's first reaction was to put a stop to the meetings. Susanna, however, held her own and argued that Samuel would be risking the wrath of God on his own soul if he forced her to neglect the people by ending this ministry. Samuel raised no further objections and the meetings apparently continued until his return.

Susanna died in 1742, seven years after her husband. Throughout her life she held a dominate place of influence in John Wesley's life. He often sought her counsel on matters of spiritual direction and always held her in the highest regard. She was one of the first to persuade him of the value of lay preachers in the revival movement he led. Some even speculate that her kitchen meeting plan was the forerunner of the ingenious class system utilized by Wesley during the revival. Susanna lived her last years in accommodations at the Foundery, the London headquarters for the emerging Methodist movement. Although an Anglican, she was buried in Bunhill Fields, the Dissenters cemetery located near the Foundery.

Home Life

Susanna Wesley is sometimes referred to as the true founder of the Methodism. This is due in part to the strict code of life, conduct, and spiritual development that she enforced in the Wesley home. She believed a parent's first task was to subdue the child's stubborn will and bring him or her into a mindset of obedience to parents. Signs of rebellion, tantrum, selfishness, or disobedience were never tolerated. However, Susanna knew better than to insist on discipline at the expense of wisdom. She believed children should never be punished for honest mistakes or failing to perform a task well so long as their intent was to please or obey. If a child was guilty of an offense, they were to be spared any severe punishment if they readily confessed their guilt and made amends for the wrong. When punishment was required, no child was ever to be punished twice for the same misconduct.

Formal home schooling began on the child's fifth birthday. The first day's assignment was to learn and memorize the alphabet. The school day consisted of three hours in the morning and three hours in the afternoon. Remembering the value of her own early education, she insisted that all her daughters were taught to read and write before they were taught to do housework. And even then, they were to spend as many hours each day in reading as they did in housework. Certainly a revolutionary concept of female education for the time.

Susanna's weekly schedule for a private hour with each of her children has become well known. Monday was for Molly, Tuesday for Hetty, Wednesday for Nancy, Thursday for John, Friday for Patty, Saturday for Charles, Sunday for Emily and Sukey. (Samuel Jr. was apparently already away from home at this point while Kezzy was either an infant or not yet born, thus explaining their absence from the schedule.) These were times for tender talks about religious questions, spiritual issues, and personal development that the children seemed to anticipate and enjoy. This strong commitment to her children formed a bond with them that lasted throughout her life.

Although Samuel was often away from home or busy with his pastoral duties, it would be false to assume that he was a disengaged father. In fact, he too was involved in the education of his children, especially in the more scholarly subjects. Although his instruction would have been primarily for the sons in order to prepare them for university studies, the girls would have had at least some exposure. It is known, for example, that as a young child Hetty learned Greek and Latin from her father. Together, Samuel and Susanna, along with help from hired servants, ordered the busy Wesley home on a rhythmic routine. Children's lessons in the morning from 9am to noon and in the afternoon from 2 to 5pm. Family prayers and supper at 6pm. Washing the children at 7pm. Bedtime at 8pm.

The fire that destroyed the church parsonage in 1709 stands as the most dramatic event for the Wesley family during their Epworth years. On the night of February 9 the family was awakened to find their home engulfed in flames. Five year old John slept through the excited evacuation and was not missed until it was too late. Trapped on the upstairs level of the old timber frame house he was given up for dead. Suddenly, he was spotted standing at his bedroom window. With no time to retrieve a ladder, one neighbor climbed on the shoulders of another neighbor in order to reach him. John was snatched from the window just as the flaming thatched roof collapsed into the room. The dramatic rescue left a permanent impression on both John and his mother. They saw it as a sign of God's unique blessing and calling on his life. Thereafter he often referred to himself as "a brand plucked from the burning" (Zechariah 3:2).

Brothers and Sisters

The Wesley's were a large family. Susanna gave birth to nineteen children, though nine died in infancy. Of the remaining ten there were three sons and seven daughters. John was the fifteenth of the original nineteen and the second of the sons. All three sons followed in the tradition of their father and grandfathers by enrolling at Oxford University in preparation for ministerial orders.

Samuel Jr. was the first of the Wesley children. Although he did not speak his first words until the age of five, he turned out to be exceptionally intelligent. Susanna commented that his remarkable memory made him a rapid learner. At the age of fourteen he was sent to Westminster School in London. There he distinguished himself beyond even the expectations of his mother. Next came Oxford, from which he graduated in just two years. He then returned to Westminster School as a teacher and began his lifelong career as an ordained school teacher and administrator. Being thirteen years older than John and seventeen years older than Charles placed him in the position of being a surrogate father to both brothers during their own school days in London. John attended Charterhouse School while Charles followed Samuel to Westminster School. Much to the relief of Samuel and Susanna, he was able to keep a close eye on John and actually taught Charles. Samuel was happily married and the father of two children.

Charles was next to the youngest Wesley child. His steps to eventual Anglican ordination followed directly the path of his eldest brother–Westminster School and Oxford University. Though much closer to John in age and relationship, his personality and gifts seem to have been much more like Samuel Jr. The main difference between Charles and Samuel Jr., however, was their view of the Methodist movement. Samuel was never a supporter of the movement, while Charles was its primary supporter. He was clearly John's closest friend, advisor, and colleague. They did, however, have serious points of disagreement, as will be seen later. Charles is best known today for his prolific hymn writing. His poetic work still provides the simplest expression of Wesleyanism's theological foundation and spiritual passion. Charles too was happily married and the father of three children. Both of his sons displayed signs of musical genius before they could read. The oldest, Charles Jr., became one of the world's most famous organists of his time.

Unfortunately, the stories of the seven Wesley sisters are not so happy. In fact, they were often tragic. The reasons stem from a combination of factors, including the isolated location in which they grew up and the limited options available to eighteenth century women. The only respectable employment open to well bred young women such as the Wesley girls was teaching in private schools or serving as governess in the home of a wealthy family. However, marriage and motherhood was always the ultimate goal since it was society's standard of measuring status. Although the Wesley family enjoyed a certain degree of social prestige, their lack of wealth greatly hindered the marriage prospects for the daughters. Their plight was further aggravated by the remote rural location in which they lived. Simply stated, most men of the region were illiterate and uncouth. The Wesley girls, on the other hand, were educated and refined. Their dilemma was obvious. They lacked the wealth to attract suitable prospects from far off places of high society, but they were too cultured to match compatibly with the local men. The results were often painful.

Emilia, known as Emily, was the eldest daughter. Though eleven years older than John, the two of them were close throughout life. She left home as a young woman with the hope of finding employment in London as a governess. There she met and fell in love with Robert Leybourne, an Oxford educated acquaintance of her brother Samuel. She did not, however, find employment and had to return to the family home in Epworth. She continued to correspond with Leybourne until she was forced by her mother to end the relationship. The reasons are not known, but it appears that Samuel Jr. did not approve of Leybourne and may have influenced Susanna's view of the relationship. Emily went on to become a school teacher and eventually married at the age of forty-three. She was apparently widowed fairly soon afterward. For much of her adult life she lived in a state of poverty and bitterness. In her later years, however, she joined the Methodist work in London and became noted for her spirit of compassion and kindness to suffering people.

Three years younger than Emily was Susanna, nicknamed Sukey. Like Emily, she spent some time in London before returning to her home area. At about the age of twenty-four she married a wealthy land owner, a local man named Richard Ellison. The marriage quickly became a nightmare. Ellison turned out to be a crude and cruel husband. He lost his fortune and physically abused his wife. In spite of this Sukey stayed with Ellison and produced four children. Eventually, however, she could no longer bear her miserable lifestyle and left her husband. Little is known of her later life. She died in 1764 at the home of one of her daughters.

The next daughter was Mary, or Molly to the family. The misfortunes of Molly's life were of an entirely different nature. As an infant Molly somehow suffered a serious injury which permanently affected her physical development. Small and partially disabled, Molly's prospects for either marriage or independence were very dim. In spite of this, she was in many ways the brightest source of joy among all the Wesley children. She was known to be a happy, loving, and witty child. Although she is reported to have once said, "I have been the ridicule of mankind and the reproach of my family,"[4] there is no specific evidence of unkindness or mistreatment toward her. The sad words most likely reflect the way she viewed herself. Molly never expected to marry. However, when her father brought a young assistant named Johnny Whitelamb into the Wesley home, friendship quickly became romance. Johnny became an Anglican minister and married Molly in 1733. Less than a year later Molly died during childbirth.

The most troublesome of the Wesley children was the daughter called Hetty, whose given name was Mehetabel. Hetty was known to be exceptionally bright and attractive. By the age of eight or nine she was reading scripture and other literature in Greek and Latin. She was a lively, fun-loving girl, but she was also prone to mischief and poor judgment. She was a popular young woman who drew the attention of many young men. She eventually eloped with a young lawyer (whose true identity has never been resolved) after her father refused to approve of their plans for marriage. By the time she realized the man had no real intentions of marrying her, she was already pregnant. Samuel was furious and unforgiving. Their broken relationship was never fully healed. With her life in ruins, a marriage was hastily arranged with a local illiterate plumber named William Wright. This husband turned out to be as cruel as Sukey's husband. Until Wright's death several years later Hetty lived in a world of abuse and unhappiness. Her circumstances improved in widowhood, but the sad outcome of her life was always seen as a great tragedy. One of the less complimentary aspects of Wesley's life is the fact that he remained largely unsympathetic toward Hetty and did not attend her funeral.

Next in the line of daughters came Anne, whose nickname was Nancy. Very little information about her has survived. It is known she worked for a time as a governess and then married John Lambert, a land surveyor. Anne and John seem to have enjoyed a happy marriage and a respectable life. There was one period of trouble when financial problems forced them to temporarily live with the Wesley parents. The only complaint registered against Lambert by any of Anne's family was his fondness for drinking with his brother-in-law, William Wright (Hetty's husband). Anne had one son, but his fate is unknown.

---

4   Arnold Dallimore, *Susanna: The Mother of John and Charles Wesley* (Durham: Evangel, 1992) 134.

John Wesley was born one year after Anne and then three years after John came the sixth daughter, Martha. She became known as Patty within the family. The most serious minded of all the daughters, she was noted as the only Wesley who had no sense of humor. She was, however, very loving and very much loved. Many prospective husbands sought her attention, but the one she fell in love with was a young clergyman named Westley Hall.

Hall had been a student of her brother John at Lincoln College, Oxford, as well as a member of the Holy Club. However, he turned out to be anything but a model of what the Holy Club stood for. Patty met Hall while she was living in London and they quickly became engaged. Later, when visiting Epworth, he met and became attracted to Patty's sister Kezzy. Revealing nothing to Kezzy of his engagement to Patty, he indicated to John that God had made it clear to him that he was to marry Kezzy. Then, after returning to London, he announced that God's latest revelation was for him to marry Patty after all. Yet he once again indicated to Kezzy his intention to become engaged to her. Then, within a matter of days, he married Patty.

In spite of the strange sequence of events with Hall, the two sisters seemed to have maintained a close relationship. Hall, on the other hand, continued in his tendency toward bizarre behavior. He fathered several illegitimate children and eventually abandoned all pretense of being a Christian, though John believed he returned to a true experience of repentance and faith before his death. For her part, Patty remained faithful and loving throughout. She gave birth to ten children; but only, a son, survived infancy, though he too died as a teenager. Patty was a woman of remarkable character. She lived to the age of eighty-five and died four months after her famous brother John. They share the same grave at City Road Chapel in London.

The last of the Wesley children was Kezia, called Kezzy. She apparently suffered from bouts of poor health throughout her life and died at the age of thirty-two. Her only known romantic interest was the strange adventure with Westley Hall. Although John stated that she was brokenhearted over the affair, Kezzy gave no indication of having taken it all that seriously. There were some hints of a relationship with another unnamed man, but lack of specific information leaves it only in the realm of speculation. She was particularly close to Charles, the sibling nearest to her in age. He was with her at her time of death and reported that she passed away peacefully with a thankful and loving spirit.

With the notable exception of Charles, none of the other Wesley siblings became leaders of the later revival movement that bears the Wesleyan name. However, their lives do provide insights into the culture and ideals of their time. Even more significantly, their stories allow a glimpse into the inner workings of the home from which John Wesley came. The high value placed on piety, intellect, loyalty, and discipline were principles that he carried throughout his life. However, an honest assessment of the Wesley family can not help but raise questions about some aspects of their home life. Susanna was undoubtedly devoted to her children, but was she as affectionate as she was stern? Samuel was proud of his clerical sons, but what of his daughters? And why did so many of the Wesley children struggle as adults to find love and acceptance, both from romance and from God? In many ways the Wesleys were an exceptional family. In other ways they were just an ordinary eighteenth century English family coping as best they could with the demands of an often difficult life.

The Young Scholar

Charterhouse School

At the age of ten and a half John Wesley left the familiar comforts of Epworth for the city of London. Through his father's connections with people of high society he was nominated by the Duke of Buckingham for a place at Charterhouse School. Boarding school education was the usual preparatory path to one of England's two universities at Cambridge and Oxford. Wesley's seven years at Charterhouse seem to have been a positive experience for the most part. His home background instilled in him the ideal qualities for boarding school—studious, disciplined, and sociable. He did well in his studies and was particularly liked by the schoolmaster. He also followed his father's advise for keeping healthy by running around the school yard three times each day.

There were also points of struggle for the young Wesley. He had to endure the usual bullying that older students inflicted on younger ones. This included taking the younger boys' ration of daily meat, which sometimes left John to go hungry. He also wrote years later that this was a period of spiritual decline. He read the Bible and said the prescribed morning and evening prayers, but he was negligent of other spiritual practices and routinely fell into acts of sin. Although none of these deeds were scandalous by the world's standards, he knew they were still sin. By this early stage of life Wesley was already fighting the battle that would consume him for the next twenty years. He craved the assurance of genuine saving faith while living in the reality of nominal faith. While still at Charterhouse he had come to place his hope for salvation on three things: "1. Not being so bad as other people. 2. Having still a kindness for religion. 3. Reading the Bible, going to church, and saying my prayers."[5]

John's older brother, Samuel Jr., was teaching at Westminster School just two miles from Charterhouse. They saw one another frequently and Samuel monitored John's progress closely, which he duly reported back to their father. It was probably Samuel Jr. who determined when John was ready to make his bid for a place at Oxford. However, it was Samuel Sr. who had the connections to facilitate those ambitions. He arranged an interview for John with Dr. Henry Sacheverell, a highly influential acquaintance. The interview did not go well. In fact, it barely happened at all. Sacheverell took one look at the undersized teenager and promptly dismissed him as being too young to have possibly learned Greek and Latin yet. Wesley said nothing, but inwardly he seethed with resentment, fully confident that he already knew more Greek and Latin than the distinguished doctor. In fact, according to Samuel Jr., John was also progressing well in his studies of Hebrew by this time. Fortunately, there were others who could verify John's readiness for university and he was awarded a scholarship for Oxford in 1720.

Christ Church

Wesley arrived in Oxford shortly after his seventeenth birthday. He was admitted to Christ Church, the largest college of Oxford University. The college had been founded by Cardinal Wolsey in 1525 and then refounded by King Henry VIII in 1546. By Wesley's time it had risen to a prominent position of wealth and power. Christ Church Cathedral, the seat of authority for the Anglican diocese of Oxford, was located on the east side of the college quadrangle and served as the college chapel, as it still does today.

The universities of Oxford and Cambridge were male only institutions that still retained much of their ancient monastic character. Everyone, students and faculty alike, were required to be unmarried members of the Church of England. Almost all teaching was done by clergymen. The two universities provided the country with its supply of clergy, lawyers, politicians, and medical doctors. Strong loyalty to church and crown were expected, though there were voices of dissent on both counts. The Christian heritage of the universities was under particular threat from the rising popularity of deism and skepticism.

Deism was the belief in an impersonal God who was too far removed from his creation to have any form of interaction with it. In practical terms this meant that Deism sought to strip Christianity of its beliefs in divine

---

[5] *Works* 1:98.

miracles, divine revelation, and the orthodox understanding of the incarnation. Skepticism, in its simplest form, was the rejection of both faith and reason and the glorification of doubt. The growing influences of these two "isms" marked any expressions of evangelical Christianity for ridicule and abuse, especially in the elitist atmospheres of Oxford and Cambridge.

In keeping with university practices of the day, Wesley received a broad classical education in philosophy, divinity, ancient languages, mathematics, natural philosophy (science) and rhetoric. He was known as a good student with a particular flair for logic and debate. Letters to family members refer to concerns over finances and occasional health issues, but not to academic pressures. Although his scholarship provided some funds for his education, he still needed help from his parents. Susanna reassured him that he should keep focused on his studies while they worked to do what they could to assist him.

Glimpses of Wesley's social life also emerge from this period. Contrary to the image often thought of him, he was a fun loving and popular young man. A witty conversationalist, he enjoyed quoting Shakespeare, liked music, art, dancing, attending the theater, rowing, and playing games of chess, billiards, cards, tennis, and backgammon. He developed a particularly close relationship with the Kirkham family in the nearby village of Stanton Harcourt. The son, Robert, became a close friend and later member of the Holy Club. The daughter, Sally, became Wesley's first disappointment in love. They enjoyed many days together and held obvious affections for each other, but the relationship came to an end when Sally accepted the marriage proposal of a local schoolmaster. Although Wesley had no intentions of marriage at that time, he clearly felt the pain of losing Sally to another man. Proper and stoic as he was, he attended the wedding and danced at the reception.

In spiritual terms Wesley seems to have continued his practices of religious observance much as he had at Charterhouse. He attended the services, read the scriptures, said the prayers, and received communion according to the traditional requirements of the university. Yet within himself he knew there was more to be experienced than the mere form of religion. On one occasion a late night conversation with the porter of Christ Church caused him to admit "that there was something in religion which he had not found."[6] Shortly thereafter his spiritual direction took a distinctly more serious turn. Though his doubts and struggles would continue for many years yet, he was clearly persuaded of his own intent to be a real Christian.

---

[6]   Kenneth J. Collins, *A Real Christian: The Life of John Wesley* (Nashville: Abingdon, 1999) 20.

It could even be said that Wesley won his first convert around this time. He and a friend, Robbin Griffiths, were in the University Church of St. Mary the Virgin one evening discussing the funeral of a young woman with whom they were acquainted. The circumstance moved Wesley's mind to matters of spiritual importance. As they turned down one of the aisles of the church, he pressed Griffiths with a rather direct and personal question. He asked to "have the pleasure of making him a whole Christian, to which I knew he was at least half persuaded already."[7] The difference between a whole, or real, Christian and a half Christian was a distinction that would remain in Wesley's focus for the rest of his life. It was also about this time that he began to express an understanding of holiness as an inner experience of the heart rather than the outward performance of religious duty.

Lincoln Fellowship

By the time he received his B.A. degree in 1724, Wesley was casting his eye toward settling down in the academic life as a college Fellow (faculty member). This not only meant proceeding on to the MA degree, but also seeking ordination in the Church of England. After a period of deep reflection, and with the supportive counsel of his parents, he began preparations in the spring of 1725 for the ordination examinations. The following September he was ordained a deacon at Christ Church Cathedral. Two years later he completed his master's degree, and the following year he was ordained an Anglican priest, again at Christ Church Cathedral.

In 1726, Wesley was awarded the prized position he sought. With a great deal of assistance from his father's lobbying of key people, he was elected a Fellow at Lincoln College, Oxford University. Bursting with pride, Samuel is famously quoted as responding, "Wherever I am, my Jacky is a Fellow of Lincoln." In fact, Wesley's new position was more than just a matter of pride. It was also a matter of personal security with a guaranteed income and lodging for as long he remained unmarried. Most significantly, it placed Wesley in a position and status that would later serve him well as the leader of the emerging Methodist movement.

One of the attractions of an Oxford fellowship was the degree of freedom it granted its members while continuing to provide them with an annual stipend. Wesley took advantage of this allowance in 1727 to assist his father in the ministry at Epworth, which also included the village church at nearby Wroot. As Samuel's curate he had two main responsibilities. First, he was to provide general support for the parish work of the two churches. In

---

[7] *Works* 12:10.

this regard he followed closely the pattern of his father; a ministry of stern authority and high churchmanship softened with a spirit of genuine compassion and devoted service. Second, he was to assist Samuel in writing (in Latin, of course) his lifelong scholarly project–a detailed exposition of the Old Testament book of Job. This exposure to parish life was a significant experience for Wesley. After so many years of scholarly endeavors and elitist atmospheres the real world of the common, uneducated, poor parishioner was a necessary component of his maturing process.

Wesley's service with his father was short lived. After just two years he was summoned back to Oxford to assume teaching duties at Lincoln College. For the next six years (1729–35) he enjoyed the prestigious life of an Oxford don. His specific areas of teaching were Greek, logic and philosophy. However, this was no isolated existence. Momentous events were taking shape and converging in Wesley's life.

First, there was in Wesley a growing sense of spiritual focus. His study of devotional works, both classical and contemporary, deeply influenced his perception of genuine Christian faith. He commented specifically that William Law's two books, *Christian Perfection* and *A Serious Call to a Devout and Holy Life*, "convinced me, more than ever, of the absolute impossibility of being half a Christian; and I determined . . . to be all-devoted to God, to give him all my soul, my body, and my substance."[8] In spite of his best intentions at this stage, Wesley still saw salvation in terms of human effort to conform to the teaching and example of Christ.

Second, there was the arrival of his younger brother Charles in Oxford. Charles completed his preparatory training at Westminster School and enrolled at Christ Church about the same time that John was leaving Oxford to help their father in Epworth. Like many undergraduates, Charles arrived at college more interested in fun than learning. He was less studious and disciplined than John, but more naturally sensitive, artistic, and as later experiences would reveal, level-headed. He joked during his first year in Oxford that he had no intentions of becoming a saint all at once. However, when John returned to Oxford to assume his duties at Lincoln College he discovered a changed Charles. Although still jovial and popular, he had made a commitment to take his spiritual development more seriously. It was, in fact, Charles rather than John who organized the first meetings of the now famous Holy Club.

---

[8] *Works* 11:367.

The Holy Club

The organizational origins of the Wesleyan movement began with the decision of Charles to put into practice a structured ordering of his devotional life. He persuaded two or three others to join him in a commitment to partake of communion weekly and to participate in a serious-minded study group. Students William Morgan, Robert Kirkham, and John Gambold were the first to align themselves with the Holy Club, one of the earliest names of ridicule by which the group was known. Within a few months John Wesley was back in Oxford and with Charles' blessing the leadership of the group quickly shifted to the older brother. This was due both to John's more obvious leadership skills and to his status as a college Fellow. Still, Charles was always the second key figure of the group. It was Charles who first encouraged a poor student from Pembroke College named George Whitefield to join the Holy Club. Although Whitefield had little contact with John at this time, he would later emerge with John as a dominate personality in the Methodist revival.

Under John's direction the group met regularly for prayer, Bible study, and the reading and discussion of other relevant books. They also took communion weekly and engaged in social ministries to those in the prisons and on the streets of Oxford. It was this methodical demonstration of piety that gave rise to the nickname "Methodists" being applied to the group. Intended as an insult, it eventually became the common name by which the movement chose to be identified.

It is important to understand the reason behind the devout lifestyle and activities of the Holy Club. Although much good was clearly done and the motives were genuinely sincere, these early actions and efforts were not of an entirely evangelical nature. That is, the purpose of the group was not only to minister to the souls of Oxford, but to minister to themselves as well. Through deeds of self-discipline and good works the Holy Club sought first and foremost to obtain a sense of their own acceptability to God. This is in sharp contrast to Wesley's post-conversion abundance of religious and social activity, which was distinctly evangelical. After his Aldersgate Street conversion, Wesley finally realized that works of righteousness are a consequence of the assurance of salvation rather than a means of gaining assurance.

By this time Wesley was passing in age from his twenties into his thirties. During these maturing years he began to set aside many of his leisure pursuits as the more serious side of his personality developed further. By no means does this mean he lost his wit or sense of humor. He remained a popular conversationalist and party guest throughout his life. However, the focus, energy, and drive that was so characteristic of his later ministry was now beginning to emerge.

In 1734 Wesley came under pressure from his family to return to parish work at Epworth. Samuel, now seventy-one years of age, hoped John would become his permanent successor. With John as the rector Samuel and Susanna could continue living in the familiar Epworth parsonage that had been their home for so long. Charles was ineligible since he was not yet ordained. Samuel Jr. was not viable because he was already well established in his career as a schoolmaster in Devon. John felt that he too was settled in his own life and had no real desire to accept his father's plan. He agonized over the decision and even took initial steps toward acceptance, even though his heart said otherwise. He held his ground in the end and declined the Epworth offer in spite of heavy pressure from his father and older brother. Samuel died the following year and Susanna was forced into the care of her children. John assumed her full support in later years.

In fact, Wesley's life was not as settled as he may have supposed. In 1735 he became acquainted with General James Oglethorpe, founder of the Georgia colony in America. With surprising speed Oglethorpe recruited both John and Charles to leave Oxford and join him in Georgia. John was to be pastor to the colonist and missionary to the Native Americans. Charles was to be Oglethorpe's personal secretary. Although Charles had completed both B.A. and M.A. degrees at Oxford, he had not elected to pursue ordination. However, in order that he might also assist John in some pastoral duties he was pressed, almost against his will, into accepting ordination. In October 1735 the Wesley brothers boarded the *Simmonds* and sailed for America with Oglethorpe. They were accompanied by two of their Methodist associates, Charles Delamotte and Benjamin Ingham.

2

Guideposts to Aldersgate

The Georgia Missionary

Atlantic Voyage

Among the passengers of the *Simmonds* were twenty-six Moravians, a Protestant evangelical group from Germany. En route to Georgia from their community base in Herrnhut, they could never have guessed the impact they were about to have on the newly commissioned missionary to America.

Wesley had never been to sea before and he did not find this first experience to be enjoyable. The prospect of an Atlantic storm was everyone's natural fear. Nevertheless, the ever diligent cleric immediately assumed pastoral care for the ship's passengers and crew. Within days he was leading worship services and, in true Wesley style, structuring a system of regular devotional exercises. The passengers of the *Simmonds* became in effect a captive extension of the Holy Club. Desiring to converse with the German speaking Moravians, he set about the task of learning their language. The Moravian leader, Bishop David Nitschmann, followed suit by studying English.

About five weeks into the three-month voyage Wesley's fear was realized as the first of several storms struck. He was awakened by the rolling of the ship and the fierce sound of the wind, but what he remembered most was his fear of death. The worst encounter of the voyage came in January. For a full week the *Simmonds* was tossed and battered by storms. Wesley endeavored to go about his pastoral duties for the sake of others, but inwardly he was terrified. He was amazed, however, to observe how peaceful the Moravians remained throughout the ordeal. While the English passengers screamed in panic the Moravians calmly sang hymns. Later Wesley asked one of them if he was not afraid during the storm. The answer came back, "I thank God, no." Wesley pressed the issue a little further, "But were not your women and children afraid?" Mildly the man replied, "No; our women and children are not afraid to die."[1]

The importance of this experience is that it confirmed in Wesley's mind that his view and practice of religion were seriously lacking. He longed for the kind of assurance that was so remarkably present in the Moravian Christians. He longed for a faith that could instill within him that assurance of Christ's forgiveness and acceptance; that assurance that would enable him, too, to face the certainty of death without fear of the judgment to come.

The *Simmonds* finally arrived in Georgia on February 5, 1736. The mark of the Moravians, however, had been firmly impressed on Wesley. He was now convinced beyond doubt that something very significant was lacking in his own experience of religion. However, the role of the Moravians was far from over. The seed they planted on board the *Simmonds* would ultimately be harvested by another Moravian band two years later in London.

American Experience

Wesley went to Georgia with idealized hopes and expectations. He seems to have envisioned the town of Savannah to be populated by loyal Anglicans eagerly awaiting the arrival of a new minister. He was equally optimistic about his prospects for evangelism among the Native American people. He pictured them as innocent, but ignorant, souls who would quickly adopt the Christian faith once it had been logically presented to them. He would be frustrated and disappointed on both counts.

Wesley took his role as missionary very seriously. He enjoyed meeting the indigenous people and concluded that they were humble and teachable. This first impression was understandable. Chief Tomochachi had visited London and was acquainted with Christianity. He told Wesley that following his trip to England, he and his people had been eager to hear "the great Word." With the passing of time, however, they were having doubts about their initial openness. Nevertheless, he assured the missionaries that he was glad they had come. There was, however, one very clear condition: "We would not be made Christians as the Spaniards make Christians. We would be taught before we are baptized."[2] Tomochachi had a very personal reason for this stipulation— the Spaniards had killed his father for refusing Christian baptism. Although this first encounter was generally pleasing to Wesley, his early optimism soon faded. Within months he became disillusioned by the Indians' preoccupation with tribal wars and their contentment with their traditional concepts of religion. That, along with Oglethorpe's insistence that Wesley's first duty was

---

[1] *Works* 1:22.
[2] Ibid., 25.

to the people of Savannah, meant that his original ambitions of missionary evangelism were never realized.

He became more confident about the possibilities for conversions among America's African slaves, despite the fact that he never actually had opportunity to minister to them. General Oglethorpe did not permit slavery in the Georgia colony, but Wesley did meet slaves in South Carolina. Although he was later known to be an ardent opponent of slavery, his first concern was over the lack of pastoral care available to the slaves. He was troubled by a conversation with a slave girl in which he learned she went to church every Sunday, but only for the purpose of carrying her mistress's children. She heard the services but knew nothing of their meaning; nor did she receive any form of religious instruction from her master. Wesley determined that she had no concept of God at all, though she was eager and able to learn. A few days later a young male slave was sent to travel with him to another town. He wrote, "This lad too I found both very desirous and very capable of instruction."[3] Wesley concluded that with only a little cooperation from the plantation owners there could be a viable ministry among the slave population.

Although his ministry to the colonists enjoyed a view bright spots, the overall work with his fellow Europeans did not go well. He was certainly a picture of good intentions and hard work, even learning Spanish and Italian along with his newly acquired German in order to converse with a wider range of immigrants. Still, the American adventure was a mismatch. He was accustomed to working with the poor and illiterate in his native Lincolnshire and in the prisons and streets of Oxford; but the immigrants to Georgia were another type of people altogether. Many were debtors who had been deported from English prisons. Even those who had immigrated by choice often had less than noble reasons for leaving England. The town of Savannah had been established only three years before Wesley's arrival. His new parish was rough, primitive, and uncultured by English standards.

Wesley's approach to Savannah's citizens did not help the situation. His years of Oxford scholarship, Holy Club discipline, and misguided devotion to outward piety had left him poorly prepared for leading a congregation of unruly colonists. He unwisely insisted on imposing a strict regime of religious rules and practice that only made him even less popular in the community. His application of the principles of the Oxford Holy Club had been dutifully accepted on board the *Simmonds* by the mild Moravians. Savannah, however, was not the *Simmonds* and the free-spirited Georgians were not

---

[3] Ibid., 49.

mild Moravians. These two facts seemed to have escaped the notice of the naïve Wesley.

There were also problems not of his making. Charles found his living and working conditions under Oglethorpe to be intolerable. He returned to England after just six months in Georgia. John was consequently forced to take on some of his duties, which often left him frustrated and irritated. He was also inadvertently caught in the middle of a complex scandal of gossip and slander that involved Oglethorpe, Charles, and two women with whom Oglethorpe may (or may not, depending on whose version of the story is believed) have committed adultery. It was Wesley's relationship with Sophy Hopkey, though, that led to the most memorable stories of his Georgia experience.

Sophy was an eighteen-year-old young woman (actually seventeen when they first met) to whom Wesley paid particular attention. She seemed sincerely devout and gladly accepted Wesley's personalized instruction and counsel. Although Wesley was in his early thirties they grew close and romantic feelings became evident on both sides. Wesley fell in love. Unfortunately, he did not know what to do with his feelings. At times he indicated they were engaged, but then at other times he indicated they were not. His uncertainty was not due to any wavering of his feelings for Sophy, but over questions of his own suitability as a candidate for the married life. He finally decided against marriage for two reasons. First was his conviction that he must fulfill his mission to evangelize the Indians before he would be free to marry. Second was his fear that his love for Sophy might overshadow his love for God and divert him from his religious duties. In other words, he seemed worried that the happiness of marriage might actually cause him to fall short in his pursuit of salvation.

Sophy also contributed to the puzzle of their relationship and the problems that followed. She clearly had strong feelings for Wesley, but sent mixed messages of her own. Sometimes she seemed to be waiting for a marriage proposal, but at other times she indicated that she was not available for marriage. She told him she had previously promised another man, Mr. Mellichamp, that she would marry him or no one else. She then went on to state that she now had no desire or intention of marrying Mellichamp, but could marry no one else.[4] Wesley apparently concluded that she was committed to remaining single. Thus, from Wesley's perspective, the termination of any further thoughts of marriage between them was seen as mutually agreeable. Wesley was devastated a short time later when Sophy suddenly announced her en-

---

[4] Reginald W. Ward and Richard P. Heitzenrater, eds., *The Works of John Wesley*, Bicentennial ed. (Nashville: Abingdon, 1988) 18:438.

gagement to yet another man, Mr. Williamson, and then married him just three days later.

As in his earlier experience with Sally Kirkham, he once again felt the sting of lost love. This time, however, he had truly been in love and he felt he had been deceived and wronged. The episode became a public controversy when Wesley humiliated the now married Sophy by publicly barring her from communion at a worship service. He cited pastoral reasons for his action. According to the laws of the time, parishioners were to register with their minister one day in advance of receiving communion. If the minister knew of any unconfessed sin he was to counsel the person accordingly. The parishioner could then receive communion only after a public declaration of repentance. Wesley barred Sophy on both counts. She had failed to register in advance and, in his view, she needed to repent of her deceitful actions toward him. Sophy and her new husband saw Wesley as a jolted lover who sought revenge through the rigid application of a legal technicality. They decided to respond in kind. Sophy's husband filed a lawsuit and her uncle, the Chief Magistrate of Savannah, pressed charges.

A Humble Departure

Ten complaints of petty offenses were registered against Wesley. The first charge was that he had written and spoken to Sophy after her marriage without her husband's consent. He denied the charge. The remaining nine complaints dealt with points of church law and practice rather than civil law. Wesley admitted fault on only one complaint—that he had once baptized an infant who had only two sponsors rather than the required three. Preparations got underway for a court trial to resolve the charges. Although it was apparent that nothing serious was going to come of the charges, Wesley decided it was time to leave Georgia. On December 2, 1737, he posted a public notice and informed Sophy's uncle of his intent. He planned to leave at noon but was delayed by a court action demanding that he post bail, which he refused to do. In consequence, a court order was issued to all officials that he was to be prevented from leaving the area. Mindful of his clerical duties to the very end, he remained in Savannah long enough to lead the service of Evening Prayers before slipping away after dark. His ministry in America was over after one year and nine months.

He traveled north in difficult conditions with three other men. After getting lost at one point in the swamps, they finally arrived in Charleston, South Carolina. On December 22, Wesley boarded the *Samuel* and began the voyage home. Again he had to face Atlantic storms and his fear of death. He also had to face the storm that was churning in his own heart. He used the crossing to reflect on his experience and spiritual condition. His most poignant journal entry came on January 24, 1738: "I went to America to convert the Indians; but Oh! Who shall convert me?"[5]

Back On English Soil

Passing Ships

During his first year in Georgia, Wesley had urged George Whitefield to join him in America. By the end of 1736 Whitefield had decided to accept the challenge of ministering in this new environment. In February he met General Oglethorpe, who was back in London. The decision was made that he would sail for Georgia with Oglethorpe as soon as possible. Oglethorpe, however, repeatedly delayed his departure. It was nearly a year later when Whitefield finally sailed out of London, without Oglethorpe. Wesley's abrupt retreat from Savannah meant that he had not been able to inform anyone in England of his action. Whitefield, therefore, was unaware that as he was preparing to leave England, Wesley was en route to England. Likewise, Wesley knew nothing of Whitefield's impending departure. Wesley set foot on English soil at Deal on February 1. Just eighteen miles to the north at Margate, Whitefield was on board the *Whitaker*, which sailed out into the English Channel the following day.

Upon realizing the situation, Wesley sent Whitefield a message urging him to return to London. Whitefield replied with his reasons for wanting to continue on to Georgia. In the end they had to accept the disappointment of missing each other by a single day.

There was also a deeper issue that emerged in this incident. In spite of his two year absence from England, Wesley still thought of himself as the leader of the Holy Club with a real sense of spiritual responsibility over the other members. He was stung by Whitefield's refusal to obey his call to return to London. For his part, Whitefield was hurt that Wesley had made no effort to come see him in the brief window of opportunity that had been available before his ship reached the open sea. This was just the first of a long list of disputes between the two friends that would characterize their sometimes stormy relationship for the rest of their lives.

Wesley traveled on to London where he had other matters to face. He was still under the authority of Oglethorpe and the Georgia Trustees. By returning without their knowledge or permission he was technically guilty of deserting his post. However, gossip had crossed the Atlantic faster than

---

[5] *Works* 1:74.

Wesley's ship and the trustees had heard the rumor that he was coming. Wesley immediately made his presence known and appeared before them three different times. He painted a dismissal portrait of the Georgia situation and defended his position in the events that had transpired.

Actually, Wesley's ministry in Georgia was not the total failure it is sometimes imagined to have been. Although he clearly made mistakes and stirred significant opposition, he also had supporters. Attendance at the various weekly services actually grew during his tenure. The fact that he was able to create a successful Methodist society at Savannah indicates that there were points of positive influence and result. Whitefield even sent a glowing report of praise from Georgia for the great amount of good that he discovered Wesley had done. In light of Whitefield's well known reputation for extravagant oratory, however, his report has not always been taken too seriously. In spite of all the problems, Wesley himself was able to recount a few genuinely good results of his stormy time in Georgia. He wrote, "All in Georgia have heard the word of God. Some have believed, and begun to run well. A few steps have been taken towards publishing the glad tidings both to the African and American heathens. Many children have learned 'how they ought to serve God.'"[6]

After hearing Wesley's reports and investigating the events that transpired during his ministry, the Georgia Trustees found there was plenty of blame to share. They concluded that Wesley had acted unwisely in some regards, but was not guilty of any legal offense. At worst he was viewed by at least some of the trustees as an unusual man who possessed an odd mixture of piety and hypocrisy—an assessment with which Wesley himself may have agreed at that time. Much more severe criticism was directed at Sophy's uncle, Thomas Causton. He was found to bear the greater degree of blame in the whole episode and to be guilty of mismanaging his office of Chief Magistrate. Wesley was finally able to put Georgia behind him.

Reunion and Rejection

Wesley was eager to be reunited with Charles and the rest of the little Methodist band. Charles was so shocked at hearing that his brother was back in England that he refused to believe it until John appeared at the London house where Charles was lodging. In spite of his own disastrous experience in Georgia, Charles was planning to return to the colony. In fact, John even talked briefly of returning, but with both brothers now together again in London all thoughts shifted to developments in England.

---

[6] Ibid., 83–84.

George Whitefield had become the most prominent member of the Holy Club during Wesley's absence. This was at least part of the reason why he chaffed under Wesley's directive to return to London rather than going on to Georgia. He had graduated from Oxford, been ordained, and was emerging as a strong leader in his own right. Most importantly, he had experienced an evangelical conversion and was passionately preaching wherever he could gain a hearing. Though only in his early twenties, he was becoming a national celebrity through his theatrical preaching style. He was still a member of the Oxford band, but he had also become an independent minded evangelist who no longer saw himself as a subordinate to John Wesley.

Wesley was pleased to learn that during his absence the Holy Club had begun to spread to various locations. Most of the members of the original Oxford group had moved on to other places. Some took with them the principles and practices they had learned under Wesley and formed small groups of their own. A dozen or so adherents were found to be meeting in London at the home of James Hutton, an old Oxford friend. However, it was Whitefield's popular preaching that did the most to draw wider public recognition to the group that was now becoming known as the Methodists. He formed a small but dedicated society at his hometown of Gloucester, which turned out to be the first permanently functioning Methodist society. With Whitefield's work at Gloucester and his growing national fame, Hutton's leadership in London, and the return of both Wesley brothers, the fledgling Methodist societies were ready to expand.

The scattered movements of the original Holy Club members had left the Oxford society largely disbanded. Charles made at least some attempt to revive the remnant group, but apparently without much success. John returned to find only three men still committed to the Holy Club ideals. He immediately set about strengthening the society and reviving its activities. He visited friends, preached in the Castle prison and Bocardo jail, and met with the society to teach and lead prayers. Soon the Methodists were once again a dynamic presence in Oxford with a total of approximately one hundred people actively involved in two or three societies. Oxford always held a prominent place in Wesley's heart and remained a frequent stop in his extensive travels. Although he grew increasingly exasperated with the spiritual state of the university, he loved the city and held his Lincoln College Fellowship until he was married in 1751.

Wesley was still a few months away from his famous conversion experience, but he was already a changed man in many regards. He fully recognized that his own spirituality lacked the peace and holiness that he read about in the scriptures and saw in the lives of others. In spite of his many years of resolve to be a *real* Christian, he was the first to admit that he had fallen far short. In some sense, however, he had already come to believe intellectually what he was still waiting to realize in experience. On his very first Sunday back in England he preached in London at St. John the Evangelist's Church "on those strong words, 'If any man be in Christ, he is a new creature.' I was afterwards informed many of the best in the parish were so offended that I was not to preach there any more."[7] A week later he preached at St. Andrew's in Holborn with similar result, "Here too, it seems, I am to preach no more."[8]

Such rejection was to become a familiar response to the man and his message. In fact, those first two Sundays back in England were just a mild prelude to the heated, and even violent, responses that would come later. Personal rejection by friends or colleagues was always painful, but rejection of the biblical message of real Christianity by "the best in the parish" was a different matter. Wesley was not one to be easily intimidated. From the very beginning he wore such treatment as a badge of honor. Not because of his naturally stubborn personality, but because of his conviction that this was genuine persecution for biblical truth. In the future he would need more than mere conviction of doctrinal correctness to endure sustained mistreatment. He would need the transforming power of a personal encounter with the Christ he was endeavoring to proclaim.

Moravian Mentors

August Spangenberg

An understanding of Wesley's journey to conversion requires a glance back to one of the most positive aspects of his time in Georgia. On just his second day there he met August Spangenberg, the Moravian pastor in Savannah. When Wesley discerned that Spangenberg was of the same spirit as the Moravians he had met on the *Simmonds* he immediately sought his spiritual counsel. Spangenberg began the interview with two pointed questions: "Have you the witness within yourself?" and "Does the Spirit of God bear witness with your spirit, that you are a child of God." Wesley was unprepared for such questions and had no answers. Spangenberg saw Wesley's confusion and tried a different question: "Do you know Jesus Christ?" After yet another pause Wesley finally answered, "I know he is the Saviour of the world." To which Spangenberg replied, "True, but do you know he has saved you?" Again Wesley skirted the issue by responding, "I hope he has died to save

---

[7] Ibid., 84.
[8] Ibid.

me." Finally Spangenberg brought the point home: "Do you know yourself?" Wesley said, "I do."

Wesley was clearly shaken and baffled by the conversation. Yet upon reflection he knew the episode had exposed his weak and uncertain spiritual condition. He admitted in his *Journal* entry that his answer to the last question was not true, "I fear they were vain words."[9] Undoubtedly, Spangenberg was of the same opinion.

Wesley remained strongly attracted to the Moravians. He even lived with them for several weeks while waiting for his own house to be vacated. He admired their calm lifestyle and pious devotion as models of what the early church would have been like. When he witnessed a Moravian ordination he was deeply moved by its simplicity. The setting was so much in keeping with his picture of the early church that he said he could easily have imagined Peter and Paul presiding over the service. He observed the Moravians to be kind and gentle with one another at all times, even while living together in a single communal building. He was also intrigued by their singing of hymns, which was not an accepted practice in the Church of England. He later introduced hymn singing into the Anglican services in Georgia and produced *A Collection of Psalms and Hymns*, the first American hymnbook.

Most of all, Wesley was amazed at the sense of assurance the Moravians possessed in regards to their own salvation. While he firmly believed Jesus was the Savior of the world, he only hoped he would prove good enough to be among the saved. The Moravians, on the other hand, had no such worries. Not because of arrogance, but because of the witness of the Holy Spirit to their hearts that they were in fact forgiven and accepted by God through the work of Christ. This was the assurance Wesley desperately longed to know. In his search he even sought to join the Moravian community, but his request was denied. Spangenberg said he should not join them unless he was first expelled from his own church for holding to strong convictions of belief and practice. While that may have been part of the reason, the true obstacle was Wesley's lack of spiritual understanding and experience.

In many regards Wesley fulfilled the stereotype of a rigid and authoritarian cleric. One of his worst examples was when he refused communion to a German pastor whose baptism he did not considered valid because it had not been performed by a recognized ecclesiastical authority. In later years he shamefully referred to his behavior as the epitome of "High Church zeal."[10]

Surprisingly, there was also a different and sharply contrasting side of Wesley's character that sometimes emerged. That is, he was also willing to

---

[9] Ibid., 23.
[10] *Works* 2:160.

accept that dogmatic doctrine and personal experience do not always agree. This was a rather remarkable aspect of his nature, especially in light of his background and ecclesiastical environment. He demonstrated this unexpected side on board the *Simmonds* and in Georgia by his response to the Moravians. Their sense of assurance of salvation did not fit within Wesley's doctrinal concepts, yet he accepted the reality of their experience and yearned for it himself.

Peter Bohler

Wesley's association with the Moravians did not end with his departure from Georgia. In fact, that first acquaintance proved to be just a prelude to the very significant contacts that were to follow. One week after arriving back in England, Wesley met Peter Bohler, "A day much to be remembered," he noted in his *Journal*. [11] Bohler was a Moravian missionary who had just landed in London while en route from Germany to America. He and his two companions had not yet secured lodging so Wesley found a place for them to stay close to his own accommodation. Wesley was exuberant over his good fortune of meeting these Moravians in London and spent every available moment in conversation with them. Bohler would spend four months in England that would be of enormous consequence for Wesley.

A week after meeting they traveled together to Oxford and talked at length. However, Wesley acknowledged that, "I understood him not; and least of all when he said, 'My brother, my brother, that philosophy of yours must be purged away.'"[12] Unfortunately, Wesley did not press Bohler for an explanation of his statement. Consequently, historians have never been able to determine exactly what Bohler meant. The comment is generally taken to be a reference to Wesley's overly logical approach to spirituality. Wesley craved an experience of the heart, but he was so much a man of the mind that he only knew to approach spirituality by listing resolutions of his good intentions and the rules he would keep to fulfill them.

Over time Wesley began to gain an understanding of Bohler's view of faith and salvation. Wesley had always thought his spiritual unrest was due to a deficiency in his degree of faith. He reasoned that troublesome issues like lack of peace, scarcity of joy, absence of assurance, and most of all, fear of death would be overcome if only he could generate enough faith by adhering to a demanding religious routine. Bohler quickly perceived, however, that Wesley's problem was not a lack of the right degree of faith, but a lack of true faith at all. Just as Spangenberg had seen two years earlier, Bohler now

---

[11] *Works* 1:84.
[12] Ibid., 85.

saw that Wesley had faith *about* Jesus, but he did not have faith *in* Jesus. He had no problem believing that Jesus was the Savior of the world, but he had never been able to actually believe that Jesus was *his* Savior. Bohler finally convinced him that the kind of faith he was seeking did not exist in degrees. He either had it or he did not. He either believed Jesus was *his* Savior, or he did not. If the response he had previously given to Spangenberg, "I hope he has died to save me," was the best he could offer, then he was still in a state of unbelief.

On March 5, 1738, Wesley admitted that he was "clearly convinced of unbelief."[13] By this he acknowledged that Bohler had persuaded him of the biblical teaching that salvation only comes by faith in Christ. This was a colossal step for Wesley, but it still left him with an old problem and also a new one. The old problem was that even though he now accepted the theological correctness of the doctrine of salvation by faith, he still did not possess that faith. The new problem was that he felt he could no longer preach to others since he was in a state of unbelief himself. He asked Bohler if he should stop preaching until he had this faith. To his surprise, Bohler emphatically told him to keep preaching. Wesley says, "I asked, 'But what can I preach?' He said, 'Preach faith *till* you have it; and then, *because* you have it, you *will* preach faith.'"[14] This then became his course of action.

The next day Wesley presented this new doctrine of justification by faith alone to a condemned prisoner in Oxford. He admitted that Bohler had previously tried to get him to speak to this man about his need of salvation before dying. He declined on the grounds of his long held conviction that deathbed acts of repentance were motivated by fear rather than genuine sincerity, and therefore, deathbed conversions were impossible. This was just one of many previous assumptions that Wesley would eventually set aside. A few weeks later he again preached at the Oxford Castle prison and prayed with another condemned man.

> He kneeled down in much heaviness and confusion, having no rest in his bones, by reason of his sins. After a space he rose up, and eagerly said, "I am now ready to die. I know that Christ has taken away my sins; and there is no more condemnation for me." The same composed cheerfulness he showed, when he was carried to execution: And in his last moments he was the same, enjoying a perfect peace, in the confidence that he was "accepted in the Beloved."[15]

---

[13] Ibid., 86.
[14] Ibid.
[15] Ibid., 90.

With experiences such as this and his continued conversations with Bohler and others, Wesley became convinced not only that salvation came through faith alone, but that salvation could come instantly to the one who believed. This concept of instantaneous conversion was another shocking discovery for him. At first he argued against this point. Then, in yet another example of his willingness to learn from experiences that seemed to contradict his theoretical doctrine, he conceded that he could not refute the valid testimonies of the many people he had come to know who gave personal witness to this experience. On April 23, he wrote, "Here ended my disputing. I could only cry out, 'Lord, help thou my unbelief!'"[16]

On the first day of May 1738, Wesley traveled to London to visit Charles, who was ill at the home of James Hutton. In the course of the visit Charles let it be known to John that he was strongly opposed to this new doctrine John was preaching. In reality, Charles was just as miserable in his spiritual state as John. He too had for some time been in a desperate search of his own for peace in his heart. He was ill much of the time and may have been suffering a nervous breakdown.

That evening a small group from Hutton's Methodist society gathered at the house. They were to meet with Bohler for the purpose of working out some guidelines that would give them a sense of structure as a society. Wesley's presence was accidental since he had not even planned to be in London at the time. After this organizational meeting the society subsequently met at Fetter Lane. The newly established Fetter Lane Society would be the focal point of Methodist activity in London for the next several years. Three days after the meting at Hutton's home Bohler left for America, but not before persuading Charles also to accept the validity of the doctrine of salvation by faith.

Strangely Warmed

An Evangelical Conversion

Wesley's moment of triumph came in London on May 24, 1738. The culmination of years of study, struggle, good intention, and discontent finally arrived. After attending the service of Choral Evensong at St. Paul's Cathedral he reluctantly decided to go to a nearby Moravian society meeting.

> In the evening I went very unwillingly to a society in Aldersgate Street, where one was reading Luther's preface to the Epistle to the Romans. About a quarter before nine, while he was describing the change which God works in the heart through faith in Christ, I felt

---

[16] Ibid., 91.

my heart strangely warmed. I felt I did trust in Christ; Christ alone for salvation: And an assurance was given me, that he had taken away *my* sins, even *mine*, and saved *me* from the law of sin and death.[17]

With great joy Wesley testified to the group of the faith and assurance that had suddenly come to him. The celebration continued after the meeting when Wesley and several others walked a short distance away to the house of John Bray where Charles was still recovering from illness. Charles received the news of John's conversion with great enthusiasm, for he too had come to the very same experience of saving faith just three days before.

The significance of Wesley's Aldersgate Street experience is monumental. It is the pivotal point of his life and the Methodist movement. Without it the names of Wesley and Methodism would likely be nothing more than obscure footnotes in the pages of church history.

But what actually happened at Aldersgate? Was this truly a Christian conversion or was it just an awakening to what was already present? It certainly was not conversion in the sense of moving from no religion or some other religion to Christianity. He was, after all, an ordained Christian minister. And his years of disciplined piety, hard work, and deep convictions make it difficult to accept that he was just a superficial Christian who was converted to a deeper level of sincerity. Yet to class the Aldersgate experience as just a change of perspective on the matter of assurance falls short as well. The confusion over the exact nature of his conversion is not without some warrant. Wesley contributed to the problem himself by later drawing a distinction between the faith of a servant and the faith of son. In his mature years he concluded that he had possessed the faith of a servant before Aldersgate. This has been interpreted by some to mean that he actually was already a Christian before Aldersgate. Also, Wesley added notes to later editions of his *Journals* which seem to reflect uncertainty in his own mind about the exact nature of his pre-Aldersgate state.

The ambiguity over Aldersgate is at least in part because it can be seen as a combination of all the above. It certainly contained elements of awakening and assurance, but it is equally certain that it included much more. His transformation from works-oriented religion to grace-oriented faith was in fact a true conversion to biblical Christianity. The radical nature of this transformation is further highlighted by his recurring references to the freedom from sin that he had come to know. In a letter to his skeptical brother Samuel on October 30, 1738, he gave his definition of what it means to be a Christian and how that related to his Aldersgate experience:

---

17 Ibid., 103.

By a Christian, I mean one who so believes in Christ, as that sin hath no more dominion over him: And in this obvious sense of the word, I was not a Christian till May the 24th last past. For till then sin had dominion over me, although I fought with it continually; but surely, then, from that time to this it hath not;—such is the free grace of God in Christ.[18]

The term "Evangelical Conversion" has become the most common modern way of referring to the Aldersgate encounter. Although it is not a term ever used by Wesley, it does help to clarify his experience. The term is used in reference to the experience of the New Birth, which involves forgiveness of sin, justification by faith, and regeneration of heart and life. Whatever else may be said of Wesley's pre-Aldersgate faith, it is certain that it was not a faith that understood and accepted the evangelical concept of Christianity. Wesley's post-Aldersgate faith, however, clearly does embody these qualities. Prior to Aldersgate Wesley was already converted in the "Catholic" sense of having turned from the world to God. After Aldersgate he was converted in the "Protestant" sense of experiencing saving faith.[19]

Ups and Downs

At the time, Wesley clearly saw Aldersgate as his conversion to real Christianity. He had accepted Bohler's belief that there were no degrees of faith, though he would later reject that notion. This view of faith, along with the profound difference that he actually did experience within his spirit, convinced him that he had never actually been a Christian prior to that moment. However, he was also confused. Bohler had taught him that when this faith came he would be free from sin, doubt, and fear. In their place he would find the love, peace, and joy of the Holy Spirit, or "happiness and holiness" as Bohler called it. Wesley immediately realized that all of this did not actually happen to him.

Temptation was the first problem to arise. In fact he had no sooner returned home than he "was much buffeted with temptations; but cried out, and they fled away." He quickly discovered that this was to be a frequent pattern. Temptation still came, but when he called upward, "He sent me help from his holy place. And herein I found the difference between this and my former state chiefly consisted." Formerly he had tried to fight sin and temptation through his rigorous piety, but now he discovered the strength of calling on Jesus. He saw that in the former mode "I was sometimes, if not often,

---

[18] *Works* 12:33.

[19] Kenneth J. Collins, "Twentieth Century Interpretations of John Wesley's Aldersgate Experience: Coherence or Confusion," *WTJ* 24 (1989) 19–20.

conquered"; but in the new mode, "I was always conqueror."[20] This then was the first surprising discovery that deviated from his expectation: being a *real* Christian did not mean exemption from temptation. Temptation still came, but there was power from the Holy Spirit to repel it. A short time later he would learn that the key to dealing with temptation was not to stand and fight against it, but to flee from it altogether, thus avoiding its full weight of influence.

The second problem to confront Wesley's new faith was lack of joy. His *Journal* entries contain repeated references to the peace that reigned in his heart after Aldersgate, but he was clearly concerned over the absence of joy. This does not mean he was unhappy. It is rather a reference to the state of spiritual ecstasy that he had expected to experience. His first impulse was to revert back to his old ways. He thought perhaps he could induce this joy by spending more time in prayer. He invested in a day of prayer to pour out his heart to God, but the next morning "I waked in peace, but not in joy."[21] Eventually he would learn that joy, in the sense he was expecting to experience, was not always overtly demonstrated. There would be times of joy, but joy would not be evident at all times.

As appealing as the notion may be that Aldersgate instantly transformed the spiritually feeble Wesley into a victorious saint, it is not true. On the one hand he knew a profound spiritual event had occurred in his heart, but on the other hand the resulting consequences did not measure up to what he had been led to expect. Yes, he was genuinely changed, but he did not feel entirely victorious. The days following Aldersgate were crucial to his still evolving understanding and development. In a very real sense Aldersgate threw him into a new state of spiritual turmoil. Not the former chaos of striving to achieve a higher degree of faith, but rather a struggle to make sense of his new faith.

It was a full year before the transformation that began at Aldersgate was complete. In the meantime his thoughts and feelings were subject to fluctuations. This was something later recognized as common to even the most committed Christians. For the most part he was fulfilled and energized by his walk with Christ. Yet there were occasional dark days of doubt and fear. These were often punctuated by desperate and exaggerated declarations that he was still not a Christian at all. However, a *Journal* entry from October 1738 best reflects his true state of thinking in the months following Aldersgate. There he discussed in what senses he was and was not a new creature in Christ. In terms of his judgments, designs (intentions), conversations,

---

[20] *Works* 1:103–4.
[21] Ibid., 104.

and actions he concluded that he was a new creature. However, in terms of purity of desire, love for God, and abiding joy he concluded .hat he was not yet a new creature. But the final statements of this self-examination reveal the very important progress that he was making in his understanding of biblical faith. In spite of his points of spiritual weakness, he possessed a settled trust that he was in fact accepted, forgiven, and "reconciled to God through Christ."[22] This was an affirmation of faith he could never have made prior to Aldersgate

---

[22] Ibid., 161–63.

3

Innovations and Disappointments

Beginning of Evangelical Ministry

Pilgrimage to Herrnhut

IN THE summer of 1738, Wesley decided to travel to Germany to visit the Moravians of Herrnhut. He had been so impressed by the group while in Georgia that he wanted to see their home community firsthand. Although that was still part of his motive, it was no longer his only motive. By this time Wesley was beginning to develop a sense of unease over Bohler's teaching that faith does not exist in degrees. This view had influenced him greatly in the days leading up to Aldersgate. However, two compelling sources of authority–his own experience and the Bible itself–seemed to be telling him something else. He hoped a visit to Herrnhut and counsel with its leaders would resolve his questions.

Wesley and several companions left London on June 13. Traveling by sea and river where possible and over land when necessary, their first destination was Marienborn, the home of the Moravian leader, Count Nicholas Ludwig von Zinzendorf. They arrived at Marienborn on July 4 and stayed with Zinzendorf for two weeks. Wesley's German was too rusty to use fluently so the conversations were held in Latin and English.

His talks with Zinzendorf produced the first of several surprises that contradicted what he had been taught by Bohler. Zinzendorf allowed that justification and assurance were not necessarily linked in time. That is, one could put saving faith in Christ and be forgiven, but not receive assurance until sometime later, perhaps even much later. This was in direct opposition to Bohler's view. Furthermore, Zinzendorf held that the evidences of justification, such as peace and joy, were not always present. Sometimes they would be apparent, but often they would not.[1] Wesley was already moving toward these views himself, but at the time his confusion was actually heightened by Zinzendorf.

Wesley finally arrived at his ultimate destination of Herrnhut on August 1. Over the next two weeks he immersed himself in the life of the Moravian community. He took extensive notes on all aspects of what he heard and saw. He was especially careful to record detailed accounts of his interviews with several individuals as to their spiritual experiences and understandings. Here he received even more mixed and confusing signals. Some testimonials and viewpoints agreed with Bohler's positions while others differed. If nothing else, Wesley learned that the Moravians were not as theologically unified as he had supposed.

As much as Wesley admired the Moravians, there were difficult moments, as when he was barred from taking communion with them. Although the reasons are not entirely clear, it was apparently because his questioning spirit left doubts in their minds as to the exact state of his salvation. He also developed reservations about certain aspects of their organizational structure and leadership. He even noticed that in both their daily routine and their religious observance they sometimes tended to be petty, superficial, and lighthearted.

In spite of these disappointments and the fact that Herrnhut did not provide the concrete answers he hoped for, still the pilgrimage was a treasured event. Wesley was strongly attracted to the concept of Christians of like faith living together in an orderly community. As in Georgia, he found the Moravians of Herrnhut to be loving and peaceful. After two weeks he reluctantly departed, noting that "I could gladly have spent my life here."[2] Upon later reflection, however, he would conclude that the Moravians were not such an ideal people after all, and were in fact in error on several points of doctrine.

Out of the Church, into the Fields

Soon after returning from Germany, Wesley was pleased to welcome George Whitefield back from America. Although Wesley was the leader of the Methodist movement, Whitefield was still the more prominent figure in the eyes of the public. Whitefield immediately resumed his popular preaching activities and within a few months was engaged in the irregular practice of open air preaching near Bristol. Whitefield did not invent open air preaching

---

[1]   Richard P. Heitzenrater, *Wesley and the People Called Methodists* (Nashville: Abingdon, 1995) 82–83.

[2]   *Works* 1:120.

(it had been known on a small scale in previous times), but he did popularize it and use it to an extent never seen before.

After several weeks of field preaching in Bristol, Whitefield wanted to take his evangelistic efforts to Wales where an evangelical revival was already underway. On March 3, he wrote to Wesley about the marvelous opportunity for ministry to the Kingswood coalminers and mildly suggested that Wesley come. He followed three weeks later with a second letter specifically requesting that Wesley come within days to replace him in the fields.

Wesley was not overly enthusiastic about the idea. Not only was open air preaching irregular, it could also be dangerous. He consulted with Charles and others at the Fetter Lane Society in London. Charles was at first utterly appalled at the thought. Finally, with some degree of reluctance, they all agreed he should go to Bristol. Wesley left London on Thursday, March 29, and the following Sunday watched Whitefield as he preached in the fields. His well known *Journal* entry reflects his state of discomfort with what he saw: "I could scare reconcile myself at first to this strange way of preaching in the fields . . . having been all my life (till very lately) so tenacious of every point relating to decency and order, that I should have thought the saving of souls almost a sin, if it had not been done in church."[3]

Whitefield left for Wales that very evening and put the open air ministry in Wesley's hands. The next day, "At four in the afternoon, I submitted to be more vile, and proclaimed in the highways the glad tidings of salvation, speaking from a little eminence in a ground adjoining to the city, to about three thousand people."[4] With that event the whole of Wesley's future ministry took a significant turn. Although he was already growing accustomed to being excluded from church pulpits, his ministry with the societies was still viewed as civil and respectable. Now he had crossed a line. He was breaking cultural norms and ecclesiastical tradition. Those things, however, quickly became secondary when he saw the ministry potential of following through with what Whitefield had started. In just one afternoon from a small hill near Bristol he had preached to three thousand people. Few church buildings in England could hold such a crowd. And even if they could, people like the coalminers of Kingswood would not likely be in the congregation.

Once again the presuppositions of theory gave way to the realities of experience. Wesley had found a surprisingly comfortable niche in a very unlikely place. For the next fifty-two years he would take the gospel to the people wherever they were. Eventually he would feel more at home preaching from a hillside, a market cross, a wooden crate, and even his father's grave-

---

3   Ibid., 185.
4   Ibid.

stone, than he would from the pulpit of the university church at Oxford. He would preach from the open air to hundreds of thousands across England, Wales, Scotland, and Ireland. In 1748, he was more convinced than ever of the value and validity of this preaching. Defending its practice against critics who complained that such preaching was indecent, Wesley wrote, "The highest indecency is in St. Paul's church, when a considerable part of the congregation are asleep, or talking, or looking about, not minding a word the Preacher says. On the other hand, there is the highest decency in a churchyard or field, when the whole congregation behave and look as if they saw the Judge of all, and heard him speaking from heaven."[5]

In spite of his small physical stature, Wesley turned out to be well suited for outdoor preaching. Biographer A. Skevington Wood provides an excellent summary of Wesley's open air abilities.

> Wesley's own voice was clear as a bell, and endowed with unusual carrying powers. After preaching once on Brown Hill, Birstall, he asked someone to measure the ground, for he had noticed that some of his hearers were sitting on the side of the opposite ridge. It was no less than eighty-four yards. Yet no one had missed a word he said. At St. Ives one windy September day, he was afraid that the roaring of the sea might drown his voice. But he was enabled to make everyone hear. . . . At Chapel-en-le-Frith, the miller near whose pond the congregation was standing, tried to drown Wesley's voice by letting out the water with a tremendous gurgle, but even that failed to prevent the people hearing. Yet all this was achieved without undue strain or shouting. Wesley repeatedly warned his preachers against the perils of "screaming."[6]

A revival movement was already beginning to spread in both Britain and America. Whitefield was clearly the principal British figure at the start. However, he also felt drawn to America. He made numerous preaching tours there and became equally famous on both sides of the Atlantic. These periods of absence from England allowed more attention to be turned to Wesley. Wesley could not be said to have started the great revival movement that swept England, but his early embracing of field preaching had much to do with his rapid rise to prominence as the central leader of the British revival.

---

[5] *Works* 2:113.
[6] A. Skevington Wood, *The Burning Heart: John Wesley, Evangelist* (Grand Rapids: Eerdmans, 1967) 154–55.

Growing Pains

The Whitefield Disputes

Wesley and Whitefield first met in Oxford when Wesley was teaching at Lincoln College and Whitefield was a student at Pembroke College. Whitefield came under Wesley's influence when he joined the Holy Club. Though Wesley was older by about ten years, their mentor–disciple relationship developed into a deep friendship. They were both strong personalities with unique and complementary ministry skills. There was, however, a significant difference between them which resulted in a great deal of friction and the eventual splitting of the Methodist movement. Whitefield was a Calvinist while Wesley was an Arminian. Both strands were present in the Church of England among both laity and clergy.

As a Calvinist, Whitefield held that God had predestined the elect for salvation and that all others were eternally lost. Furthermore, those who were thus chosen were eternally secure in their salvation. Since their salvation was God's decree there could be no such thing as backsliding from salvation. Wesley, as an Arminian, held that salvation was freely offered to everyone. Only those who refused to accept God's offer would be lost. Furthermore, believers could later forfeit their salvation by choosing to revert back to unbelief. The reasons behind the opposing views of Calvin and Arminius will be explored in chapter 6.

The friction between Wesley and Whitefield surfaced shortly after Wesley's first field preaching venture at Bristol when he published a sermon on free grace. Whitefield responded by publishing *A Letter to the Rev. Mr. John Wesley in Answer to His Sermon entitled "Free Grace."* The point of their debate was not just doctrinal; it had very practical implications for ministry. Wesley argued that the doctrine of predestination made preaching worthless and vain. If God had already selected those who were to be saved, what was the point of preaching? Whitefield countered with the argument that since only God knows who the elect actually are, they had a responsibility to preach to everyone in order to awaken the elect to the good news of their salvation. Besides, argued Whitefield, there was practical value in preaching even to the non-elect if it helped to deter them from greater acts of sin and improved the quality of society.

Whitefield's charge against Wesley was that he denied God's sovereignty by giving human beings a part to play in their own salvation. Wesley countered that even in the Arminian view God is still the sole source and means of salvation. It was God's sovereign choice to give humanity the freedom to accept or reject salvation. In one sense people do have a part in their salvation, but only because God has decreed that they should.

There was also disagreement over the doctrine of Christian perfection. Whitefield believed sin remained in the Christian and that subsequent sinning in word, thought, and deed was inevitable. Wesley maintained that after being freed from the guilt of sin through justification, Christians could go on to experience freedom from all willful sinning through sanctification. He did not mean the believer could not sin, but that the believer did not have to sin, and as a normal course would not sin.

Wesley and Whitefield debated their differences in conversations, letters, sermons, and publications. The two branches of Methodism, which came to be known as Calvinistic Methodism and Wesleyan Methodism, managed to coexist for a time. Eventually, however, the old friends parted ways and led their own respective groups. In the long run the Arminian brand of Methodism flourished and spread around the world while Calvinistic Methodism remained relatively small. This was due in large measure to Wesley's superior organizational skills in his development of the Wesleyan movement.

Despite their differences, Wesley and Whitefield always considered each other dear friends. Even during the periods of heated exchange when the friendship aspect was genuinely strained, they maintained mutual respect and Christian confidence. Each sometimes invited the other to preaching opportunities. Later, when Wesley went through his most disappointing episode of lost love, it was Whitefield who stayed at his side and gave him comfort. One never questioned the other's sincerity of faith or conviction. They just disagreed on what they both perceived to be crucial points of doctrine. Whitefield died in 1770 at the age of fifty-five while in America. All of Britain mourned for him, but the chosen preacher for his London memorial service was John Wesley.

Separation from the Moravians

Wesley's relationship with the Moravians became increasingly fragile after his visit to Herrnhut in the summer of 1738. He had noted at the time several rather mild concerns and disagreements with them. Within weeks of his return to England he decided the issues were more contentious than he had first realized. He composed a letter outlining what he saw as their major faults, but he did not send the letter. He simply filed it away as a record of his thoughts at that point. The passing of time, however, did not lessen his concerns.

His unease was further heightened by events that were developing at the Fetter Lane Society. In October 1739, a Moravian named Philip Molther arrived in London from Germany. Though supposedly en route to America, he remained in London for nearly a full year. He joined the Fetter Lane Society and quickly moved into a position of influence. He convinced several members, whom Wesley regarded as strong in the faith and full of good works, that they were in fact not Christians at all. Furthermore, he said, they should no longer participate in any means of grace, including prayer, Bible reading, and communion. The only path to true religion, according to Molther, was stillness. That is, doing nothing of any outward good while waiting patiently for saving faith to arrive according to God's own timing. To do anything beyond waiting was to seek salvation through works. This became known as the stillness controversy.

James Hutton, Wesley's long-time friend and early leader of the society, had recently returned from a visit with the Moravians in Germany. He wanted to move the society toward a closer tie with the Moravians and, therefore, gave support to Molther. Wesley argued passionately against Molther's stillness doctrine for the next nine months, but ultimately without success. On July 16, 1740, Wesley was banned from further preaching at Fetter Lane. The society had determined to set its future course in Molther's direction. Wesley and nearly twenty others publicly withdrew from the society on July 20. The decision to leave was reinforced two days later when Wesley received a letter from Germany. Having been written before the events in London were even known, it "advised my brother and me, no longer to take upon us to teach and instruct poor souls; but to deliver them up to the care of the Moravians, who alone were able to instruct them."[7]

The break from the Fetter Lane Society did not necessarily mean the end of the relationship between Wesley and the Moravians as a whole, but it did eventually come. Little more than a month after leaving Fetter Lane, Wesley was engaged in a lively debate with Zinzendorf in London. Their theological differences were spelled out and clarified. Wesley later published seven points on which they disagreed in *A Short View of the Difference Between The Moravian Brethren (so called) and the Rev. Mr. John and Charles Wesley.* In essence the seven points came down to differing views on the nature and meaning of sanctification and Christian liberty. Wesley complained that the Moravian position promoted antinomianism—a doctrine that denies the value, purpose, and necessity of good works in the Christian life. His introduction to the essay reveals how strongly he felt about the matter. There he very bluntly called the Moravians "the most dangerous of all the Antinomians

---

[7] *Works* 2:283.

now in England," and stated that the purpose of the publication was to warn the "simple of heart against being taken by those cunning hunters."[8] In the end, it was Zinzendorf who officially terminated the Moravian relationship with the Wesley brothers in 1745.

Despite his sometimes rocky association with the Moravians, Wesley's attitude remained much as it did with Whitefield. He always held a genuine affection for them. Even after the disappointments of Herrnhut, the stillness controversy at Fetter Lane, and the confrontations with Zinzendorf, he still wrote fondly in his *Journal* entry for April 6, 1741: "I had a long conversation with Peter Bohler. I marvel how I refrain from joining these men. I scarce ever see any of them but my heart burns within me. I long to be with them; and yet I am kept from them."[9]

Opposition from Church and Society

Wesley spent most of his ministry in what many would consider an impossible situation. He was following a call and leading a movement that inevitably left him vulnerable to pressure from all sides. Within the Church of England he struggled to maintain an extremely delicate balance. He adamantly held to the essential points of Anglican doctrine and polity in order to avoid separation. However, he also pushed every boundary to its limit in order to maintain the freedom that he needed. Likewise, he had to strike a similar balance within the Methodist movement, but in a different sense. Here he promoted both a message and a method that implied distinction from the established church, while at the same time holding back the reins of those who wanted to pursue that implication to its logical conclusion. Furthermore, there was the matter of dealing with the culture as a whole. On the one hand he sought to break the norms of society by taking the gospel to people where they lived and worked. On the other hand he needed to avoid unnecessarily alienating the very society he sought to serve and transform.

Opposition emerged as soon as Wesley returned from Georgia and then grew quickly after Aldersgate. It was not just his message that stirred up hostility. There were also problems with his method. First, there was the simple matter of his appearance. The custom of the day was for proper gentlemen to wear powered wigs. Wesley, however, had decided years earlier that he could save the cost of both wigs and barbers by simply letting his own hair grow long. Critics viewed this as a display of vanity rather than pious frugality. Second, there was his preaching style. Fairly early in his ministry he began preaching without reading from a manuscript. The freedom of movement

---

[8]   *Works* 10:201.
[9]   *Works* 1:306.

and expression that this allowed him to incorporate into the sermon was considered uncouth and unprofessional by many. Third, and most controversial of all, was his practice of praying extemporaneously rather than reciting prescribed prayers. Such informality of conversation with God was deemed offensive and wholly inappropriate. On these points, however, Wesley was not to be deterred. He saw them as valid principles of authentic Christianity for which he was willing to stand.

His methodology stirred further problems simply because it was in many ways unorthodox. His self-styled mode of itinerant preaching was met with strong resistance by both clergy and civil authorities. It seemed a blatant violation of the laws that forbade preaching in any parish area without prior approval from the local clergyman. Wesley countered this view with two arguments. First and foremost, God had called him to preach whenever and wherever the need was to be found. This extraordinary call was the primary basis for his famous declaration, "I look upon all the world as my parish." [10] His view was also supported by a second argument. He maintained that his status as a Fellow of Lincoln College gave him legal authority to teach and preach anywhere within the realm of Great Britain. Still, not all of his opponents were convinced of the legality of his itinerancy.

Efforts to stop him by excluding him from church pulpits proved futile. In fact these actions actually served his purpose even better in some regards. In *A Farther Appeal to Men of Reason and Religion*, Wesley recalled that it was the closing of church doors that ultimately forced him into field preaching. When churches first barred him he settled for just preaching at the small gatherings of the Methodist societies. "But after a time, finding those rooms could not contain a tenth part of the people that were earnest to hear, I determined . . . to preach in the open air." [11] This public arena gave him access to huge crowds numbering in the thousands rather than the one or two hundred that could fit in a typical English church.

Wesley and his fellow preachers frequently endured mistreatment, insult, loss of property, personal injury, and even more. William Seward, a close preaching associate of Whitfield, became the first Methodist martyr when he was beaten to death.[12] Throughout the episodes of opposition Wesley maintained Christian grace and dignity. He took trouble and violence in stride, even when seriously threatened with death, as in an anti-Methodist riot at Wednesbury. He was often willing to match wits with those who would verbally abuse him, but he endured all as an act of love and witness for Christ.

---

[10] Ibid., 201.
[11] *Works* 8:112.
[12] Heitzenrater, *Wesley*, 116.

Wesley even managed at times to find humor in his persecution. While preaching from the steps of the market cross in Bolton he was pushed off two or three times, but simply climbed back and continued on. Finally, some hecklers resorted to throwing stones. At the same time, three others who intended to harass him were climbing on the cross behind him. As Wesley tells the story:

> One man was bawling just at my ear, when a stone struck him on the cheek, and he was still. A second was forcing his way down to me, till another stone hit him on the forehead: It bounded back, the blood ran down, and he came no further. The third, being got close to me, stretched out his hand, and in the instant a sharp stone came upon the joints of his fingers. He shook his hand, and was very quiet till I concluded my discourse and went away.[13]

One of the most curious accusations laid against Wesley was that he was a Roman Catholic in disguise. Charges of "Popery," as it was commonly called, followed him for most of his life. Eighteenth-century England was highly distrustful of those who adhered to Catholicism. The reasons were political. England lived in constant fear of invasion from other European powers, especially Catholic controlled France. Any prominent Englishman who was Roman Catholic was viewed as a possible threat to national security. The suspicion was that such a person might be secretly plotting with France to give the English throne to Prince Charles Stuart. "Bonnie Prince Charlie," as he was mockingly called, was the grandson of the former English king, James II. He lived in France, but claimed to be the rightful monarch of England. He did in fact attempt an unsuccessful invasion in 1745.

Wesley obviously had no connections with either France or Catholicism. Some of the efforts to portray him as a Catholic were nothing more than rumors intentionally spread by opponents who wanted to discredit him in the eyes of the public. A story circulated that he had been born and raised in Rome. One woman claimed that Wesley had taught her to pray to the saints and the Virgin Mary. She further asserted that this was a secret teaching that was not generally known. George Whitefield is reported to have later diagnosed the woman as a "lunatic."[14]

The charges of Popery usually stemmed from misunderstandings of Wesley's theology and lifestyle. The rituals of Catholicism caused many to regard it as a religion of salvation by works. Likewise, Wesley's belief that Christians should receive communion frequently and engage in good works

---

[13] *Works* 2:114.
[14] David Butler, *Methodism and Papists: John Wesley and the Catholic Church in the Eighteenth Century* (London: Darton, Longman and Todd, 1995) 33.

caused many, especially Calvinistic opponents, to regard Methodism as a religion of salvation by works. That common perception of both groups led many to conclude that Methodism was a new brand of Catholicism.

Although the Church of England authorities watched Wesley with a wary eye, it must also be noted that they actually treated him with considerable restraint. No formal charges or actions were ever taken against him. His evangelical movement was regarded on the whole with a respectable degree of patience and tolerance—most likely in the hope that it would simply die out and go away. But in spite of the church's less than enthusiastic view of Wesley's ministry, it has been suggested that the Methodists could have been embraced and legitimized within the Church of England if Wesley had been more flexible in his leadership.[15]

Heartbroken Again

In August 1748, Wesley became ill at Newcastle in the north of England. He was nursed back to health by a thirty-two-year-old widow named Grace Murray. They had been acquainted for a number of years and Wesley knew her to be a very devout woman. She served as a Methodist class leader and worked as a housekeeper at the Methodist orphanage. During his recovery he fell in love with her and in a short time was hinting toward marriage.

The following spring Grace accompanied Wesley on a preaching tour of Ireland. She proved to be the ideal ministry partner and traveling companion. It seemed the forty-six-year-old bachelor had truly found his soul mate. He was aware that she had previously been engaged to John Bennet, one of his Methodist preachers, but she gave no indication of continued interest in or contact with Bennet. While in Ireland their love deepened and they pledged marriage to each other in a formal agreement that was often accepted by the customs of the time as an actual marriage. George Whitefield, for example, was one who did consider them to be married. Wesley and Grace, however, apparently both understood it to be an engagement. In keeping with the rules agreed to by the Methodist leaders, Wesley had to first obtain the approval of his brother and agreement from the Methodist societies as a whole before he would be free to marry. He also insisted that they receive Bennet's consent. Grace gave him one year to secure these conditions.

Problems developed soon after they returned to England. Grace revealed to Wesley that she still had affectionate feelings toward Bennet. Although claiming to love Wesley far more, she vacillated between the two. Meanwhile, Charles received word of his brother's engagement and immediately set out

---

[15] John Kent, *Wesley and the Wesleyans: Religion in Eighteenth-Century Britain* (Cambridge: Cambridge University Press, 2002) 52–53.

50

from Bristol to stop it. He was adamantly opposed to the marriage, apparently because he had doubts about Grace's true character. There is also speculation that he thought the lower-class housekeeper was beneath the social status of the now famous Methodist leader. In any event, he was very angry with John for so recklessly risking a damaging scandal by proposing marriage to a woman whom Charles regarded as already engaged to Bennet.

In the midst of a situation that was already complicated by misunderstanding and confusion, Charles deliberately interfered. He convinced Grace of her obligation to marry Bennet since she was engaged to him first. He then personally took her to Bennet and saw to it that they were married a few days later. Some scholars say Charles actually performed the wedding ceremony, but Bennet's own journal says they were married "by the Revd Mr. Bruister, curate of St. Andrews Church in New Castle."[16]

It was George Whitfield who broke the news to John of what had transpired. The following day the two brothers met and had a heated exchange of words. John was devastated, both by the sense of betrayal from Grace and Bennet, and by the rash intervention and accusations of Charles. The brothers would eventually mend their broken relationship, but sadly, the bond was never quite the same as it had previously been.

Bennet later left the Methodist movement. He became an outspoken critic of Wesley and contributed to the charges against him of Popery. Wesley and Grace saw each other only once after her marriage to Bennet. In their old age, years after the death of Bennet, they had a brief meeting in London that was polite and cordial.

In 1751, two years after losing Grace, Wesley abruptly and inexplicably married Mary Vazeille, a widow from London. Charles again objected, but did not interfere. The marriage proved to be unhappy for both John and Mary. The relationship was a poor substitute for the love of his life that went unfulfilled. By the time Mary died in 1781, the couple had been separated for several years. Her funeral and burial had already taken place before Wesley even learned of her death. They had no children.

---

[16]   Simon Ross Valentine, ed., *Mirror of the Soul: The Diary of an Early Methodist Preacher, John Bennet: 1714–1754* (Peterborough: Methodist Publishing House, 2002) 194.

4

Growing to Maturity

Making a Difference

Theological Identity

WESLEY'S ROLE as a theologian has often been downplayed because he did not write books of systematic theology. It is true that Wesley does not fit the category of systematic theologian in the modern sense of the word. But that does not mean he was not a serious theologian. Many of his writings are intensely theological. However, they were written for the benefit of common people rather than the scholars of church and university. Wesley was in fact a theologian in the early church sense of the word.[1] He was a deep thinker who regarded theology as a practical endeavor directed to the needs of people rather than as the mere formulation of doctrinal concepts. That is why his theological contributions appear not as academic works, but as sermons, letters, hymns, Bible study aids, and pamphlets. Wesley has been described as less of a systematic theologian than Thomas Aquinas, John Calvin, or Karl Barth, but more of a systematic theologian than Martin Luther. He fits most closely in this regard to the Anglican Thomas Cranmer and the American Jonathan Edwards.[2]

Furthermore, he is sometimes criticized for being inconsistent in his theology. The realization that he saw theology in terms of pastoral practice helps to explain this in part because it places his theological work in its proper context. It must also be remembered that Wesley's writings covered the span of a very long life. He did not wait until old age to reflect back over decades of thought and experience before committing his views to paper. His convictions developed and deepened over many decades and were published as he

---

[1]   Randy L. Maddox, "John Wesley—Practical Theologian?" *WTJ* 23 (1988) 131.
[2]   Thomas C. Oden, *John Wesley's Scriptural Christianity: A Plain Exposition of His Teachings on Christian Doctrine* (Grand Rapids: Zondervan, 1994) 25.

viewed them at the time. Those views were sometimes modified in later life. It is unfair to Wesley to characterize this rather ordinary process of change as self-contradiction. He should be commended for preserving such a detailed record of his theological development.

A Wesleyan theological identity began to emerge as Wesley clarified the differences between himself and the Calvinists and Moravians. It was an identity that hinged primarily on two essential doctrines—free grace and holiness. He understood free grace to mean that God freely offers salvation to all and freely enables all to respond to that offer. He understood holiness to mean that Christians could be freed from the bondage and necessity of continual sinning. Neither doctrine was unique to Wesley. They were both well within the standard teachings of the Church England and orthodox Christianity. But they were doctrines that had passed out of fashion as differing interpretations of key scripture passages and the influence of John Calvin (1509–64) had taken prominence.

It is worth noting that although Wesley had strong disagreements with the Calvinistic doctrine of predestination, he was not generally an anti-Calvinist. Both of his parents came from Calvinistic backgrounds and retained many aspects of that perspective. Susanna, for example, held to a modified form of Calvinism in her belief that God had in fact elected those to salvation whom he foresaw would accept Christ.[3] For many years Wesley even accepted that God had predestined some to salvation, but that all others who chose to believe in Christ would also be saved.[4] He moved away from this view around 1750.

Wesley's main objection to Calvinism was that the doctrine of predestination seemed to dismiss the value of good works and the need for spiritual growth. He saw this as deterring believers from a life of holiness rather than leading them to it. For their part, the Calvinists saw Wesley as implying that salvation and righteousness could come by human works rather than divine grace. Despite these differences and the previously mentioned disputes with Whitefield, it can truly be said that Wesley counted many Calvinists among his highly respected friends.

Wesley was a man with strong convictions on both the theory and the practice of theology. But it cannot be said that he was theologically original. In fact, he would recoil in horror from the thought of doctrinal novelty. His intent was not to draw people to new ideas, but to point people back to the old ideas; to the Christ of scripture and orthodox tradition. He was a devoted

---

[3]   Henry D. Rack, *Reasonable Enthusiast: John Wesley and the Rise of Methodism* (London: Epworth, 1992) 74, 388.

[4]   Ibid., 388.

student of the Bible, the Early Church Fathers, and his Anglican heritage. Near the end of his life he recalled, "From a child I was taught to love and reverence the Scripture, the oracles of God; and, next to these, to esteem the primitive Fathers, the writers of the three first centuries. Next after the primitive church, I esteemed our own, the Church of England, as the most scriptural national church in the world."[5] His passion was simply to reawaken his church and country to the biblical Good News that had been preached in their land for well over a thousand years.

In order to insure that his theology was thoroughly orthodox, Wesley looked to four sources of authority—scripture, tradition, reason, and experience. All of his doctrinal understandings rested on this four point foundation, which came to be known as the Wesleyan Quadrilateral.

Scripture was clearly the cornerstone and starting point of the Wesleyan system. If a doctrinal concept was in any way unscriptural then it went no further, regardless of what tradition, reason, or experience had to say. Although Wesley was an avid reader, he described himself as a man of one book. He had no question regarding the divine inspiration and authority of the Bible. He immersed himself in it. The Bible was to be read prayerfully with the aid of the Holy Spirit. All passages were to be understood within their context and taken in their simplest and most obvious sense, unless such interpretations led to absurd conclusions.

The tradition through which Wesley filtered theological ideas was primarily that of the first few centuries of the Christian church. He held the Early Church Fathers in very high regard. Their historical proximity to the time of Jesus and the New Testament church gave them a better view of the pure Christian faith. He was also equally devoted to his own Anglican heritage, which he believed to be consistent with scripture and early tradition.

Wesley was by nature a man of reason who lived in the period of history known as the Age of Reason. While he recognized that reason taken to its extreme was detrimental to religion, he did not believe reason and religion were incompatible. He maintained, in fact, that religion without reason was not true religion at all. He insisted that religious thoughts and convictions must pass the scrutiny of sound reasoning.

Experience was to Wesley the other side of the coin of reason. Each must also involve the other. Reason made religion coherent and understandable, but experience gave religion life and power. He sought to walk a fine line between the two without falling into excess on either side. The frequent charges against him of "enthusiasm" came from critics who felt he had fallen into excesses of experience. One of Wesley's greatest fears for the Methodist

---

[5] *Works* 13:272.

people was that they would someday lose the vital reality of the personal experience of knowing God.[6]

A more detailed treatment of Wesleyan theology will follow in later chapters. The point here is simply that in Wesley's quest for a proper understanding of what he called *real* Christianity, a theological identity emerged that distinguished Wesley and the Methodists from other recognized groups.

Strength in Structure

The ingenious organizational structure of the Wesleyan movement was its second distinguishing feature. This turned out to be the crucial difference between the eventual legacies of Wesley and Whitefield. Both men traveled extensively and preached to hundreds of thousands. But unlike Whitefield, Wesley took the further step of providing a structured discipleship program that gave continuity to the movement. Whitefield's zeal was for evangelistic conversions. Wesley's zeal was for cultivating converts into faithful disciples of Christ. He accomplished this by creating an interlocking system of five groups: society, class, band, select society, and penitent band.

A *society* was in effect a congregation of Methodist members. They met regularly (often several times a week) for services of hymn singing, Bible reading, prayer, and preaching. A society was comprised of at least fifty members, but the meetings were open to the public and were also attended by non-Methodists. Wesley was very careful not to cross any technical lines that would cause a society to be legally classified as a dissenting church. This primarily meant that communion could not be served and the meetings were never to be held at times that conflicted with scheduled Anglican services. Society members were strongly urged to regularly attend their local Church of England services in order to receive communion. Most of Wesley's travels were for the purpose of meeting with societies, but with societies all over the country he could not possibly attend to their ongoing operations. For this he relied on the help of circuit-riding lay preachers. Working directly under Wesley's personal training and supervision, they were responsible for several societies within a geographic region.

Each society also had a local preacher who provided daily pastoral care to the society. Some local preachers were women. Wesley was initially opposed to this idea, but his mind was changed by two factors: the practical need for more preachers and the biblical evidence that women could be

---

6   On the Wesleyan Quadrilateral, see also Charles Yrigoyen Jr., *John Wesley: Holiness of Heart and Life* (New York: The Mission Education and Cultivation Program Department for the Women's Division, General Board of Global Ministries, The United Methodist Church, 1996) 16–18.

called by God. Although women preachers were a relatively small minority, women in general were very significant to the societies in both numbers and influence. John Munsey Turner has noted that "The role of women was much wider than preaching. Their place as class leaders and spiritual supporters of the itinerant preachers must not be underestimated. The chapel became a haven for women, a counter-influence to the dominance of the pub. A new form of voluntary culture was developing which was to endure throughout the next century."[7]

A *class* was a subdivision within each society that was made up of ten to twelve members. The weekly class meeting became the true foundation of the entire Methodist organization. Whereas the primary purpose of the society meeting was worship and instruction, the purpose of the class meeting was supervision of individual spiritual growth. It contained several unique features that gave it strength and value. (1) Every society member was required to participate in a class. Joining a society also meant joining a class. (2) Each class was deliberately structured to include a heterogeneous mix of people. That is, people from different social classes, educational backgrounds, spiritual maturity levels, age groups, and sexes were placed together. (3) Class membership was not restricted to believers only. Those identified as searchers were also welcomed. (4) The meeting was characterized by personal testimonies and discussions of spiritual progress, failures, and needs. The focus was on personal experience, not biblical or doctrinal instruction. (5) The class leader spoke first and was then followed by each member in turn. (6) Membership tickets were issued. This was a simple but profoundly significant innovation that gave the often illiterate members a sense of status and dignity. The ticket was revoked if the member repeatedly failed to live by the membership commitments. (7) All members, believers and searchers alike, were required to abide by the following commitments. Things to avoid: swearing, drunkenness, buying or selling hard liquor, fighting, quarreling, returning evil for evil, and borrowing without intent to repay. Things to do: doing good of every possible sort, giving food to the hungry, visiting and helping the sick, and living as frugally as possible. Things to do voluntarily according to individual conscience: receiving communion, private and family prayer, Bible reading, and fasting.[8]

A *band* was a smaller group of committed Christians who were striving for spiritual growth. It differed from a class in that it was completely voluntary and was structured according to homogeneous groupings of age, sex, and

---

[7] John Munsey Turner, *John Wesley: The Evangelical Revival and the Rise of Methodism in England* (Peterborough: Epworth, 2002) 129.

[8] *Works* 8:269–71.

marital status. One band might be for single young adult men, while another might be for elderly widows. Band members adhered to a stricter set of rules than other Methodists. Items listed as voluntary for classes were mandatory for bands. Band members also agreed to abstain from all uses of alcohol and tobacco unless prescribed by a physician; not to wear ornamental jewelry, lace, or ruffles; and not to buy or sell on Sundays. These rules did not exist to promote a legalistic form of piety. Rather, their purpose was to promote the virtues of simplicity, frugality, and self-discipline. The goal was to encourage and strengthen holiness. Only a fairly small percentage of Methodists opted for the rigors of band membership. Each band met weekly. After an opening time of prayer or singing each band member was to speak freely and frankly about his or her spiritual state. Everyone answered the following four questions at every meeting: "What known sins have you committed since our last meeting? What temptations have you met with? How were you delivered? What have you thought, said, or done, of which you doubt whether it be sin or not?"[9]

A *select society* was the most elite group in Methodism. These were societies of exemplary men and women who were personally chosen by Wesley for leadership development. But this was not just a training society; it was in some ways an advisory council to Wesley. Members were mentored for leadership by contributing to Wesley's management of the movement. Completely contrary to all other Methodist groups, the select society had no rules, no prescribed format, and no leader. Although membership was by Wesley's invitation only, he did not lead the meetings. All members had equal status. The purpose of the group was to provide an open forum for frank discussion on issues and strategies. Even Wesley's leadership was subject to review and criticism. Although there were no official rules, the society did operate with an understood commitment to absolute confidentiality. All major decisions were ultimately made by Wesley, but he did look to the select societies for fresh perspectives and accountability.

The final classification in Wesley's system was the *penitent band*. The only thing known for certain about the operation of these groups is that they met on Saturday evenings. Their purpose was to help those who habitually failed to live up to the class requirements. This not only meant those who simply lacked self-discipline, but also included those who were truly unable to conform. People suffering from severe spiritual or behavioral problems could join a penitent band to seek counsel and support. The rehabilita-

---

[9] Ibid., 273.

tive nature of the penitent bands has been compared to today's Alcoholics Anonymous meetings.[10]

It is widely accepted that Wesley traveled some 250,000 miles and preached some 40,000 times in his ministry to and through the Methodist movement. At the time of his death the official Methodist membership of Britain and Ireland totaled 72,476. It is also known, however, that this was a relatively small percentage of the total number of people who actually participated in Methodist societies and activities. Methodist meetings were open to the public and were regularly attended by non-members. It is estimated that the actual number of Methodist adherents at the end of Wesley's life was perhaps as high as 300,000.[11]

Social Action

Concern for social welfare was a central tenet of Methodism from its inception at Oxford. The early Holy Club members were particularly taken by the need for prison ministries. Prison conditions in eighteenth century England were generally harsh, filthy, and brutal. Prisoners could be held for lengthy periods while awaiting trial and then subjected to severe punishments for relatively minor offenses. The poor were especially vulnerable in the penal system and could expect to receive greater punishment than the wealthy for the same crime. Many were condemned to death for petty theft. The Wesley brothers and the Methodist preachers became well known for their dedicated prison work throughout the country. The sight of a Methodist preacher praying with a prisoner as he was being taken to the gallows became a familiar image in cities like London and Bristol.

Wesley's early exposure to the reality of poverty seems to have permanently affected his view of material goods. In his 1760 sermon, "The Use of Money," he set forth a formula that has been repeated many times since: gain all you can, save all you can, give all you can. His point was that Christians should be hard working in order to earn, frugal in order to avoid waste, and generous in order to give away as much as possible. A noticeable impact of the Wesleyan movement on English society was the tendency of Methodists to raise their standard of living. Many discovered that by adhering to Wesley's principles and example their economic condition improved. While this was part of Wesley's intent, it was also a source of concern for him. He worried that as people became more prosperous they would become addicted to the

---

[10]   D. Michael Henderson, *John Wesley's Class Meeting: A Model for Making Disciples* (Nappanee, Ind.: Evangel, 1997) 126.

[11]   Rack, *Reasonable Enthusiast,* 437–38.

accumulation of money and possessions. He had a deep concern for the poor and an equally deep abhorrence for self-centered affluence.

Many of Wesley's contemporaries assumed he was wealthy. In fact, he owned virtually nothing. The so-called Wesley House on City Road in London was never his. It was a Methodist owned house that he used and shared with traveling preachers during his final years. He lived comfortably, but modestly, and gave away vast sums of what could have been personal wealth. He established orphanages, leased houses to homeless widows, created businesses to provide jobs for the unemployed, operated a medical clinic, provided small business loans, and raised funds for charity from members of high society.

Education was always an important priority in Wesley's concern for the poor. He founded schools in London, Bristol, and New Castle in order to provide education for poor students. The Kingswood School near Bristol was his best known venture. His vision was for a school that would education poor students to a standard of very high quality. He claimed that its graduates were better scholars than most of those from the universities of Oxford and Cambridge. Kingswood School still operates today, though no longer as a school for the poor.

Concern for the health of England's poor prompted Wesley to publish a medical book entitled *Primitive Physick: or An Easy and Natural Method of Curing Most Diseases*.[12] Although ridiculed today as a book of quackery, the book was actually based on the work of a respected physician named George Cheyne, as well as Wesley's own experience.[13] But the book must be understood in terms of its intended purpose. Wesley sought to offer free and natural remedies to the poor who had no access to professional medical care. This endeavor was actually not as unusual as it may seem. Conscientious clergymen of that era were sometimes known to act as amateur physicians for the poor. While it is obvious now that many of his remedies were worthless, his emphasis on preventative care, such as balanced diet and exercise, was well ahead of his time.

Wesley became increasingly disturbed by the issue of slavery as he grew older. He first witnessed the practice when he was a missionary in Georgia. His only comments at the time were on the prospects for evangelism among the slaves. Later, however, he became involved in the campaign to end the British led slave trade. He was repulsed by every aspect of the business. The greed that motivated it, the methods of entrapment, the inhumane condi-

---

[12]   John Wesley, *Primitive Physick: or An Easy and Natural Method of Curing Most Diseases* (London: Trye, 1747).

[13]   Ronald H. Stone, *John Wesley's Life and Ethics* (Nashville: Abingdon, 2001) 103.

tions of transport across the ocean, the separation of families, and the callous selling of human beings was almost beyond comprehension. In his 1774 publication, *Thoughts Upon Slavery*, he wrote in vivid detail of the atrocities inflicted upon slaves and asked, "Did the Creator intend that the noblest creatures in the visible world should live such a life as this?"[14] This essay is said to have been the most influential work of its kind in his day.[15] Wesley did not live to see the end of the slave trade. It was, however, at the forefront of his mind to the very end. The last letter he ever wrote was to the abolitionist leader William Wilberforce, encouraging him to carry on the fight against slavery.

The multitude of social ills in eighteenth-century England tore at Wesley's heart. He had no interest in a personalized form of religion that ignored the hard realities of life and the plight of others. His unwavering commitment to ministry at the problem level of society is what many people, Methodist and non-Methodist alike, remember most about him.

Writing and Publishing

When Wesley was not preaching it seemed he was always reading or writing, even while walking or riding on horseback. He once commented that "History, poetry, and philosophy I commonly read on horseback, having other employment at other times."[16] What he marveled at was not his ability to read and ride simultaneously, but the fact that the horses he rode rarely ever stumbled despite his lack of attention to guiding them. He concluded that the secret was in his habit of riding with a loose rein and letting the horse find its own way. When he was given a coach for his travels in later years he had it equipped with a folding desktop so he could continue to study and work on the road.

Wesley was passionate about learning and he wanted to share that passion with the world. Toward that end he established a publishing house which he kept busy for his entire life. Not only did it produce more than four hundred thousand volumes of literature, it also provided numerous jobs for needy people. His publications covered a wide range of subjects, including theology, science, medicine, education, pastoral practice, hymn books, sermons, poetry, and language study. Some of Wesley's publications were his own writings, but many were edited or abridged works of others or collections from various authors.

---

[14] *Works* 11:68.
[15] Stone, *John Wesley's Life and Ethics,* 189.
[16] *Works* 3:393.

By modern definitions Wesley was guilty of plagiarism. Much of what was produced under his name was originally the work of others. But he should not be judged by twenty-first-century publishing standards. He was a man of his own times who worked within commonly accepted rules and practices of his own time. The point of his publishing efforts was not to produce works of original scholarship, but to mass produce huge quantities of inexpensive literature on a variety of subjects. He wanted to make books available to people who were largely excluded from access to literary works. He succeeded in this by printing small books that were easy to read, convenient to carry, and cheap enough to buy.

Wesley also felt a deep sense of responsibility for the education of his preachers. He insisted that they be well informed and enlightened readers, and even self-educated scholars if possible. All ordained clergy of any denomination, according to Wesley, should be knowledgeable not only in the scriptures, but also in Greek and Hebrew, the original languages of the scriptures. He further believed they should be thoroughly familiar with secular history, geography, science, logic, church history (especially the works of the early church fathers), and the "maxims, tempers, and manners" of people (psychology).[17] Although most Methodist preachers were lay rather than ordained and lacked the formal education necessary to fulfill Wesley's ideal, still they served with a full awareness of his high expectations.

Preachers were supplied with reading materials by Wesley through his publishing house. His most famous resource was the *Christian Library*, which he published between 1749 and 1755. It contained fifty volumes of carefully edited writings on theology and devotion that Wesley considered essential for the preachers. These works came from various sources, including the early fathers and theologians from Roman Catholic, European, and British traditions. But even in this, Wesley's ultimate purpose was that preachers be equipped to understand and communicate the message of real Christianity.

Final Years

Foundations of a New Church

The creation of a new denomination was the last thing Wesley wanted. He was determined to live and die a loyal Anglican. He always saw Methodism as a renewal movement within the church. At the same time he was under constant pressure from those who wanted Methodism to formally separate. Such pressure usually came from the lay preachers who wanted to be ordained in

---

[17] *Works* 10:482–84.

order to administer communion and to function as fully recognized clergy. Wesley searched for years in an unsuccessful effort to find an Anglican bishop who would ordain his preachers. He supported the Church of England position that only bishops were authorized by scripture to ordain others for ministry. Consequently, he refused the calls of many Methodists to ordain his preachers himself.

Eventually Wesley altered his view on who had authority to ordain. That change of mind laid the foundation for the future establishment of a Methodist denomination. It was, however, events in America that forced the issue to the forefront. Methodism was taken to America in the 1760 by Irish immigrants. In 1769, Wesley sent the first two lay preachers to America. They were soon followed by two more, including Francis Asbury; but after a decade only Asbury remained. American Methodism was urgently in need of ministers. Asbury reported that due to the absence of ordained clergy thousands of children remained unbaptized and many Methodists had not received communion in years.

After considerable debate, biblical analysis, and earnest soul searching, a momentous decision was made. Wesley would ordain ministers for service in America. Two men were ordained by Wesley's hand in September 1784. At the same time, he also ordained Thomas Coke as Superintendent of the American work. Coke was already an ordained Church of England priest. The purpose of his Wesleyan ordination was to give him the status and authority to ordain Asbury and others in America.

Charles, who was not present for these proceedings, was very disturbed at the news of what his brother had done. His opposition was so strong that it caused yet another rift between the brothers. John tried in vain through several letters to persuade Charles of his rationale. The best they could finally manage was an agreement to disagree. Charles' resistance was rooted in two key points. First, he feared that John had abandoned his lifelong pledge to keep Methodism within the Church of England. He was convinced, rightly so as it turned out, that the ordination of Methodist clergy made eventual separation inevitable. Second, he disagreed with John's recent conclusion that ordination did not necessarily require the authority of a bishop. Charles thought the ordinations were invalid because he did not believe John had a scriptural or ecclesiastical basis for performing them. Charles mocked John's ceremonial act of laying his hands on Coke for ordination with a famous rhyme:

> So easily are Bishops made
> By man or woman's whim?
> Wesley his hands on Coke hath laid
> But who laid hands on him?

Methodism's first official break from its Anglican roots occurred in America in December 1784. The Methodist Episcopal Church was created with Thomas Coke and Francis Asbury as its two Superintendents. They soon changed their titles to Bishop, much to Wesley's disapproval. British Methodism retained its Anglican ties until four years after Wesley's death.

Elder Statesman

In old age Wesley enjoyed the status of a revered national figure. There were still a few critics, but he was immensely popular and highly respected. This esteemed position gave him a greater degree of influence with people of high society. He corresponded with bishops, aristocrats, members of parliament, and prime ministers on a range of issues. He wrote on social problems of the day, campaigned for fair treatment of the Methodist preachers and people, and lobbied the rich for donations to charitable purposes. He was an outspoken opponent of the American Revolution and an avid supporter of King George III.

Wesley's greatest popularity was always among the common people, even in places that once hated him. On his last trip to Cornwall in August 1789, he reflected on how different it was from earlier days. The last time he had been in the town of Falmouth he was met by a wave of opposition that he described as "an intense mob gaping and roaring like lions." But now, forty years later, "how the tide is turned! High and low now lined the street, from one end of the town to the other, out of stark love and kindness, gaping and staring as if the King were going by."[18] Five days later he preached to a crowd of 25,000 in the natural open air amphitheater of Gwennap Pit. He had to concede, however, that at the age of eighty-six his voice was no longer up to such crowds: "I think it scarce possible that all should hear."[19] The last years of his *Journal* entries are virtually filled with accounts of his extensive travels and preaching activities. Wesley had no intention of ever retiring, and he never did.

---

[18]   *Works* 4:468.
[19]   Ibid., 469.

"God is with us"

The long span of Wesley's life meant that he had to endure the grief of losing most of his dearest friends. Men like George Whitefield, Vincent Perronet, and John Fletcher all preceded him in death. It was, however, the death of his brother Charles in 1788 that was most painful. Despite their differences of opinion and the tragic episode with Grace Murray, Wesley dearly loved his younger brother. Charles had been his right-hand assistant, trusted confidant, and best friend for sixty years. Wesley was further grieved by the fact that the letter informing him of his brother's death was misdirected and reached him only one day before the funeral. He was more than a hundred miles away and could not possibly cover the distance in time.

Wesley always marveled at his good health in old age, but by the end of 1789, he was acknowledging that the effects of nature had caught up with him. Early in 1791, he admitted to being half blind and half lame. Still, he maintained a remarkable schedule of activity. He preached his last sermon on February 23, 1791. Shortly after returning to the City Road house in London he became seriously ill. Friends rushed to his side as it became apparent that the end was near. Among his last recorded words was the testimony, "God is with us." John Wesley died peacefully on the morning of March 2, 1791, at the age of eighty-eight.

Word spread quickly through the streets of London that the venerable Wesley had passed away. In order to avoid the spectacle of thousands of mourners flooding into the area to pay their respects and get a last glimpse of his body, the decision was made for a private burial. In true Wesley fashion, he was quietly buried the next day at 5:00 AM, the usual time for preaching his first sermon of the day. Six poor men of no social standing had the honor of carrying his simple coffin from the house to his grave behind the City Road Chapel.

The Wesleyan Legacy

Wesley's era of influence did not end with his death. Although there was no strong leader to take his place, the movement still spread around the world. Some of this growth was the result of deliberate missionary activity, but much of it was simply due to immigration. The Methodists were generally a loyal people who took the movement with them wherever they went. Division within the movement also accounted for some of its expansion. Methodism had already split between Calvinistic and Wesleyan (Arminian) branches during Wesley's lifetime. After his death there were further divisions within each of these groups. The Calvinistic branch made little impact outside of Wales, while Wesleyanism went on to be the standard form of Methodism. This combination of mission activity, immigration, and breakaway Methodist groups resulted in Wesley's name being carried far and wide.

Today there are dozens of Christian churches and denominations around the world that bear the name of Wesleyan or Methodist in one form or another. There are many others that emerged from the Wesleyan heritage and adhere to its doctrine but do not overtly identify themselves as Wesleyan in their church name. Their membership numbers range from a few dozen to several million. They also represent a wide range of theological perspectives, from very conservative to very liberal.

Wesley's views on the doctrines of sanctification and Christian perfection were always subject to misunderstanding and controversy. Many Methodist bodies gradually diminished or abandoned this aspect of their heritage. Others, however, did not. Those that were convinced of the doctrine and gave it primacy in their teaching came to be known in North America as the Holiness Movement or the Wesleyan–Holiness tradition. The numerous churches and denominations that identify with this movement generally tend to represent the most evangelical wing of the broad Methodist spectrum. They strongly promote Wesley's original commitment to the concepts of personal conversion, assurance of salvation, holiness of heart that gives freedom from the domination of sin, and holiness of life that results in changed behavior and lifestyle. The following chapters on Wesleyan theology represent that particular perspective.

Part 2

The Wesleyan Passion:
A Dynamic Meeting of Grace and Faith

5

The Problem of Sin

The Loss of Innocence

A Perfect Beginning

THE ULTIMATE goal of authentic Christianity, both for individuals and humanity as a whole, is freedom from sin and purity before God. The pursuit of that goal requires, first of all, a proper understanding of the nature of sin. Sin may be defined in different ways; such as, pride, unbelief, disobedience, or self-will. But any definition ultimately reveals a broken relationship with God. The fact that the relationship is broken indicates that it was once whole. This separation from God is the essence of the problem of sin.

According to Christian understanding, alienation from God is not the natural state of humanity. Human beings were originally created in absolute harmony with God. They were, in fact, created in the very image of God (Genesis 1:26-27). That does not mean humans are, or ever were, divine in any sense. God alone is divine. What it does mean is that Christianity regards human beings as thoroughly unique creatures. Of all God's vast creative activity, only human beings are said in the Bible to have been created in God's image. This divine image is present in the human race in two distinct ways. In theological terms they are referred to as the natural image of God and the moral image of God.

The *natural image* of God refers to what might be called personality or personhood. God is personal and has passed on the qualities of personhood to the human family. This includes such capacities as intellect, self-awareness, reasoning, the ability to determine one's destiny in life, memory, immortality, and the capacity for choosing between right and wrong. Many animals also display certain instinctive personality characteristics or temperament traits, but these are not the same as the divine image of personhood that God has given to people. There is no evidence that animals have the capacity for self reflection. It is quite doubtful that a cow contemplates the meaning of life or worries over how to be more popular with the rest of the herd. Such aspects of personhood are unique to the human race because they reflect the natural image of God in which we have been created.

The *moral image* of God refers to the most fundamental aspect of who God is. God is first and foremost a God of holiness. He created the first human beings in that same state of holiness, or moral purity. Although human beings were never divine, they were originally holy. This means, first of all, that Adam and Eve had no natural tendency to do wrong. Their first inclination was to do what was right and good. Second, this original holiness means they had a natural desire to obey God and to live in a perfect relationship with him. Sin was an alien concept. Disobedience was possible, but it did not come naturally. It was an act of abnormal behavior they had to learn from an external source.

Some theologians, including Wesley, also speak of a third aspect of God's image in humanity—the political image. Wesley meant by this the unique role of primacy that God gave to humanity over all other elements of creation.[1] Adam was in effect to govern the natural environment on God's behalf. This aspect of God's image enabled Adam to rule wisely and caringly over the natural world. Although Wesley treated the political image as a separate category from the natural and moral images of God, most theologians treat it as one aspect of the natural image.

There is a crucial distinction between the natural image and the moral image that must be seen in order to gain an accurate understanding of the present human condition. While the natural image is essential to being human, the moral image is not. In other words, if humanity were to lose the element of personhood (the natural image of God) they would cease to be human. They would become just another animal in the created order. However, humanity could lose the element of holiness (the moral image of God) and continue to be fully human. They would be morally flawed and doomed to domination by sin, but they would still be human. That is precisely what happened in the biblical account of the Garden of Eden.

A Tragic Choice

When Adam and Eve sinned by taking the forbidden fruit they fell from the state of purity in which God had created them. The exact nature of the Garden of Eden story has been the subject of great discussion. The issues usually center around the question of how much of the story is to be taken

---

[1]   Kenneth J. Collins, *The Scripture Way of Salvation: The Heart of John Wesley's Theology* (Nashville: Abingdon, 1997) 23.

literally and how much is symbolic. Without detouring down those roads of speculation, there are several points that do emerge from the reality of the fall.

First, the natural image of God in humanity was damaged and partially lost. Human beings retained personality, intellect, self-determination, and other characteristics that make us distinctly human. However, that natural image became tainted and flawed. Humanity would be prone to such common afflictions as mistakes, ignorance, and poor judgment. Faults that are now routinely experienced and excused as fundamental to human nature are, in fact, foreign to human nature as originally created. Human nature as it exists today is the tattered and corrupted remnant of God's natural image.

Second, while the natural image of God was only partially lost, the moral image of God was completely lost. Through their act of disobedience, Adam and Eve destroyed humanity's pure and holy relationship with God. Human beings would never again enter the world in a state of moral and relational perfection. Adam and Eve were created with an innate love for God. Everyone since has been born with an innate spirit of rebellion against God. Adam and Eve had to overcome their natural tendency toward good in order to do evil. Everyone since has had to overcome their natural tendency toward evil in order to do good.

Third, sin was not known to the human family prior to the moment of the fall. The idea of sin did not originate with Adam or Eve. It had to be introduced from an external source. That source was Satan speaking through the form of a serpent. The fact that Adam and Eve were vulnerable to temptation is significant because it proves that holiness does not mean exemption from temptation. Jesus was the only person to live a life of absolute holiness, yet even he suffered severe temptations.

Fourth, although Satan was the source of temptation, he was not the actual cause of the fall. Adam and Eve were the cause. They alone bear responsibility for their sin. The importance of this point is that sin and temptation are not the same. There is no sin in being tempted. Adam and Eve were bound to face temptation, but they were not bound to sin. They had every advantage of resistance available to them. In fact, they actually had to suppress their natural inclination toward God in order to embrace the foreign concept of disobedience.

Fifth, Adam and Eve's sin resulted in numerous practical consequences. (1) The perfect relationship with God was broken. Rather than eagerly walking with God in the garden as they had before, Adam and Eve subsequently hid from God. (2) The perfect relationship between Adam and Eve was broken. Adam no longer saw Eve as the helper and partner God had given him, but as the person to be blamed for his own sin. (3) The perfect relationship with nature was broken. Whereas Adam and Eve had lived in productive harmony with the environment, they now had to battle against certain elements of nature in order to survive. (4) Death was introduced to the human experience. God had forewarned in Genesis 2:17 that death would be a consequence of disobedience. Adam and Eve chose to ignore this warning and to believe instead that God had lied to them. (5) Adam and Eve inflicted the reality and destruction of sin upon the entire human race. The world before the fall was profoundly different from the world after the fall. What was once a place filled with peace and holiness now became a place of violence, greed, hatred, suffering, illness, and death.

Due to the fall, sin and its consequences became permanent fixtures in the world that had once been perfect. Sin was here to stay. God created Adam and Eve in his own holy image, but they produced descendents in their own fallen image. Christian doctrine refers to this fallen image as original sin.

Sin's Universal Domination

Original Sin

Romans 5:12-21 provides the primary biblical teaching on the doctrine of original sin. The actual focus of the passage is the contrast between Adam and Jesus. Whereas Adam brought sin and death into the world, Jesus brought forgiveness and life. The climax of that contrast is in verse 19, "For just as through the disobedience of the one man [Adam] the many were made sinners, so also through the obedience of the one man [Jesus] the many will be made righteous." The universal nature of Adam's sin is clearly stated throughout the passage. In fact, the passage begins with the declaration in v. 12 that "sin entered the world through one man, and death through sin, and in this way death came to all men, because all sinned."

Roman Catholics and Protestants are in general agreement on the doctrine of original sin. Both traditions derive their views from the early theologian Augustine (354–430). Augustine formulated his ideas during a period of debate with a British monk named Pelagius. Augustine believed that through Adam's sin the entire human race was contaminated with evil. This contamination destroyed the moral image of God in humanity and introduced a depraved nature of sinful inclination. Consequently, human beings are born in a sinful condition of alienation from God. Our instinctive impulse is to do wrong and commit sin. Since we have no control over this evil instinct, it is inevitable that we will sin. As Wesley put it, "man was created looking directly to God, as his last end; but, falling into sin, he fell off from God, and turned into himself. Now, this infers a total apostasy and universal corruption in man. . . . And this is the case of all men in their natural state: They seek not God, but themselves."[2]

Pelagius took a much more optimistic view of humanity that denied the Augustinian concept of original sin. He rejected the notion that the entire human race is corrupted and cursed because of Adam. Instead, each person is his or her own Adam. Each has the freedom and power to chose right over wrong. Individuals commit their own original sin when they first choose to do wrong. Wesleyans are sometimes mistakenly labeled as Pelagian because of their belief in humanity's free will. The reasons for this will be discussed in the following chapter.

Pelagianism was condemned as heresy in the fifth century. In practice, however, it has never gone away. Modern social science and western culture continue to promote its central creed. Like Pelagius, they insist that humanity is fundamentally good. It is assumed that since even the most wicked people are usually capable of some acts of goodness and love, then this must mean they are actually good people who have been wrongly influenced by external forces. According to this popular view, the answer to evil in the world is to be found in better education, elimination of poverty, improvements in environment, and positive reinforcement. However, despite the vast amounts of finance and effort that have been directed toward these issues, the evil inclinations of humanity have not diminished.

The reality of the human condition is apparent at even the earliest stages of life. Young children who are raised in the most ideal home environment still demonstrate their natural inclination toward evil. They do not have to be taught the rudiments of self-centered behavior; they are self-centered by nature. They will naturally revolt when they do not get their way, scheme to take from another child something that they want for themselves, and lie to hide the reality of their guilt. Augustine saw this sixteen hundred years ago, even in the behavior of infants:

> I have seen a baby turn pale with jealousy as it watched another infant at the breast. This is not unusual. Mothers and nurses tell me that they have their own remedies for driving out fits of jealousy. But can you call it 'innocence' when a child demands that milk be withheld from another child who would die without it, when there is plenty to go around?[3]

Augustine's point is that self-centeredness is not learned, it is present from the moment of birth. Children do, however, have to be taught and

---

[2] *Works* 9:456.

[3] Sherwood E. Wirt, *The Confessions of Augustine in Modern English* (Grand Rapids: Zondervan, 1981) 7–8.

conditioned to share, to obey, and to be honest. While it is true that some children adapt to good behavior more easily than others, the fact still remains that they must be taught. The point is that infants are not born morally pure or even morally neutral. They are born with the same inherent moral flaw that has plagued all people since Adam and Eve first introduced sin into the human family. Because of this defective condition, human beings are prone to rebel against God and to enthrone the self. Like Calvin and the Protestant Reformers, Wesley too agreed with Augustine's doctrine of original sin and the human condition.

The Eastern Orthodox branch of Christianity takes an entirely different view of sin in humanity. They recognize that Adam's sin has harmed the entire human race in many ways, but they deny the western understanding of original sin. The two traditions agree that sin and death entered the world through Adam's fall. They also agree that because of Adam's sin the entire human race came under Satan's domination. However, the eastern tradition does not recognize this domination to be what the west calls original sin.

To the Orthodox, sin's dominion simply means we are born into a world situation in which it is easy to do wrong and hard to do right. The Orthodox will even go so far as to say that the moral image of God in humanity has been damaged by Adam's sin, but they will not say it has been destroyed. Therefore, in theory, all people are still capable of living a sinless life. On the surface, Eastern Orthodoxy sounds very Pelagian. However, it is not as optimistic about human nature as Pelagianism. As Orthodox theologian Timothy Ware explains, "as a result of the fall the human mind became so darkened, and human will-power was so impaired, that humans could no longer hope to attain to the likeness of God."[4]

In the end, both the eastern and western traditions believe human sin is inevitable. The point of disagreement is on the question of why. In the western view we sin because we have lost the moral image of God. Therefore, we are born with a morally depraved version of human nature which makes it impossible for us not to sin. In the eastern view we sin because of the overwhelming presence and power of evil that we face in the world. Although we still have the moral image of God within us, it has been so badly weakened that we lack the moral strength to resist sin. However, both traditions come back into agreement on humanity's need for a Savior. Both affirm that "human sin had set up between humanity and God a barrier which humanity by its own efforts could never break down. Sin blocked the path to union with God. Since we could not come to God, He came to us."[5]

---

[4] Timothy Ware, *The Orthodox Church*, rev. ed. (London: Penguin, 1997) 223.
[5] Ibid., 225.

The concept of original sin is sometimes obscured because of the terminology used in attempting to describe it. Terms such as inbred sin, carnality, and Adamic depravity do little to clarify the doctrine. The expression "original sin" is itself vague. All too often original sin is portrayed as some kind of identifiable object or entity. Even Augustine referred to it as a disease that has infected the soul of the human race. Unfortunately, this conjures up imagines of viruses and bacteria that can be isolated and treated. Original sin is, in fact, a moral condition. It is the state of natural rebellion against God in which human beings are born. Because of the sin of the first human beings everyone since has been born morally flawed with an inherent impulse toward sin.

Inherited Depravity

One of the great mysteries of original sin is the question of inherited depravity. That is, how is this state of sin passed from one generation to the next? Or to phrase it in a slightly different way that gets to the heart of the matter; why does all of humanity have to suffer just because of Adam's sin? Why must every child be born morally flawed rather than morally good or neutral? The Bible does not answer those questions. It merely states that all share in Adam's sin. Historically there have been three major theories on the nature of inbred sin: the realistic theory, the representative theory, and the genetic theory.

The *realistic theory* takes the view that the entire human race was actually linked to Adam at the time of creation. This link was not just symbolic, but was in some mysterious sense literal. In this view all people were present with Adam in the Garden of Eden, and, therefore, all participated in that first act of disobedience. We all stand guilty of Adam's sin because it was literally our own act of sin as well.

The *representative theory* views Adam as one would view a head of government who represents a large group of people. The actions of that one person can bring either prosperity or destruction upon the whole group. According to this theory, Adam bore responsibility for the future condition of his descendents because he was the first representative of the entire human race. We all suffer because of his sin. We did not literally sin with him, as in the realistic theory, but there is still a sense in which we did sin with him because we are represented by him. Therefore, the consequences of that first sin apply not only to Adam, but to all.

The *genetic theory* takes a different view altogether. It does not see original sin as something in which we participated, but as something that is reproduced in each new generation. Just as children inherit certain physical and personality traits from their parents, so in the same way they also inherit the moral defect of original sin. According to the first two theories humans are born in sin because they actually share in Adam's sin. In the genetic theory, people are born in sin because their parents have passed Adam's sin on to them.

Calvin and most of the Protestant reformers held to the realistic theory. Since this theory sees all of humanity as already guilty of actual sin, it fits particularly well with the Calvinistic doctrines of predestination and election. If all have already sinned, then all are already condemned to eternal punishment. Therefore, God's decree of predestination, in which he elected some to salvation, is an act of great mercy and grace toward the chosen few.

Wesley was not overly concerned about the method of inherited depravity. He generally accepted it as an unanswerable mystery. In his lengthy treatise, *The Doctrine of Original Sin*, he wrote:

> If you ask me, how sin is propagated; how it is transmitted from father to son: I answer plainly, I cannot tell; no more than I can tell how a man is propagated, how a body is transmitted from father to son. I know both the one and the other fact; but I can account for neither.[6]

Wesley did, however, hold a definite preference for the representative theory. Just a few pages prior to the above quote, he stated that "Adam was . . . our representative; in consequence of which, 'all died' in him, as 'in Christ all shall be made alive'." However, he went on to conclude that "as neither representative, nor federal head, are scripture words, it is not worth while to contend for them."[7]

The genetic theory is not generally supported by evangelical theologians because it lacks explicit scriptural foundation. Passages like Romans 5:12-21, indicate that original sin comes to each member of the human race directly from Adam. No passages specify that it is passed from parents to children in any genetic manner.

Confusingly, both Calvinists and Wesleyans commonly use the language and images of the genetic theory when discussing original sin. That is, they both speak of it as something that is inherited and passed from generation to generation, thus implying adherence to the genetic theory. However, neither tradition actually holds to the genetic theory. This misuse of language is especially detrimental to the Wesleyan–Holiness movement, which places great emphasis on how God deals with the problem of original sin through

---

[6] *Works* 9:335.

[7] Ibid., 332.

the work of entire sanctification. Obviously, a confused perception of original sin will result in a confused perception of entire sanctification.

Total Depravity

Sometimes the terms original sin, inherited depravity, and total depravity are used interchangeably. In fact, as the previous two sections have indicated, they are related but not synonymous. Technically, original sin is the fall of Adam in which all of humanity has participated in one sense or another. Inherited depravity refers to the manner in which universal sinfulness is conveyed to all of Adam's descendants. Total depravity refers to the degree of impact that the fall has had on humanity.

Contrary to a common misperception, the doctrine of total depravity does not teach that humanity is totally bad. Adam's sin did not destroy all human potential for goodness. The moral image of God in humanity was lost in the fall, but the natural image of God was only damaged. That marred remnant of God's image still enables us to see and do some degree of good.

What the doctrine of total depravity does teach is that the depravity of sin which we all inherit from Adam affects the totality of our being. Everything about us, physically, spiritually, emotionally, and intellectually, has been scarred by the fall. Nothing is left untouched. We are totally depraved in that we are so thoroughly steeped in sin that we are completely incapable of helping ourselves. We are absolutely dependent upon divine grace, even to be enabled to call on God for help.

Wesley echoes this understanding in his sermon "On the Deceitfulness of the Human Heart." Drawing from Jeremiah 17:9 ("The heart of man is deceitful above all things, and desperately wicked"), he writes, "Hence there is, in the heart of every child of man, an inexhaustible fund of ungodliness and unrighteousness so deeply and strongly rooted in the soul, that nothing less than almighty grace can cure it."[8] This is total depravity, the tragic state in which all humans live from the moment of birth.

Depravity in Action

Personal Sin

Wesleyan theology is careful to distinguish between sin as an inherited condition and sin as a personal act. Although inherited sin has placed within humanity a fallen and corrupted nature, it is personal acts of sin that have dragged the world into a continuous spiral of hatred, bitterness, and greed.

---

[8] *Works* 7:340.

The Bible uses several different terms to illustrate the meaning of personal sin.

The most common New Testament image of sin is that of missing the mark (from the Greek word *hamartia*). It is often assumed that this means falling short of God's perfect standard. While there is certainly an element of that meaning in the concept of personal sin, it is not the most accurate image. It is more precise to say people miss God's mark primarily because they are not aiming at it. They focus on their own targets of achievement rather than God's target. The image of falling short portrays more the consequences of total depravity. The image of a wrong aim speaks directly to the issue of intentional action.

Other biblical expressions for sin include transgression, wrongdoing, ungodliness, lawlessness, and disobedience. These terms are actually metaphors that help us to see different aspects of the meaning of sin. The Bible also identifies several specific acts of sin; such as murder, theft, lying, adultery, drunkenness, witchcraft, lust, and idolatry; to name just a few. All of these are sins of commission. That is, they are sinful acts or desires in which people engage. Active sin, however, also includes sins of omission. That is, refusing to do what is known to be right and good.

The Reformed tradition has generally seen sin as any failure to conform to God's perfect standard. Since humans are fallen and imperfect, it is impossible to conform to God's standard. To be human is to be sinful, even after conversion to Christ.

Wesley understood sin differently. He penned his classic definition of sin in a letter to Mrs. Elizabeth Bennis in 1772: "Nothing is sin, strictly speaking, but a voluntary transgression of a known law of God."[9] Wesley agreed that the fall had rendered humanity incapable of meeting God's perfect standard. However, he disagreed that this inability falls into the same category of sin as willful wrongdoing. "Voluntary" is the key word in Wesley's definition. There must be conscious awareness and intent in order for an act to be sin in the sense of requiring confession and repentance. Wesleyans, therefore, do not view those who have been truly converted to Christ as sinners. They are viewed as *former* sinners who are now redeemed children of God. Although they may on occasion commit sin, that is no longer their normal pattern of life.

---

[9] *Works* 12:394.

Unintentional Sin

In spite of his emphasis on intentional sin, Wesley was aware that the Bible does make reference to unintentional sins in Leviticus 4–5. He did not see these "involuntary sins" (as he called them), however, in the same light as voluntary sins. They are indeed sinful in the technical sense of violating God's law, but they are not sins for which the offender is morally accountable. Since these sins lack willful intent, Wesley did not believe they fulfilled the scriptural definition of sin in the usual sense of the word.

One way of illustrating Wesley's doctrine of sin is to imagine a shopper who makes a purchase and unknowingly receives too much change in return. The shopper then leaves the store without realizing the error. Is this person guilty of stealing? In the legal sense he is. He has taken something which is not rightfully his. In the moral sense, however, he is not guilty because he is not aware of what he has done. A Wesleyan sees this as the crucial distinction. The shopper would not be guilty of sin, strictly speaking, since there was no willful intent. If the shopper later realizes the error and does not return the money, then it becomes a deliberate act of sin for which he needs to seek forgiveness. However, if the shopper returns the money after discovering the error then there has been no intentional sin and, therefore, no need for repentance and forgiveness.

It is especially important for Wesleyans and Calvinists to understand one another on their differing concepts of sin. The Wesleyan who hears the Calvinist speak of daily sinning in word, thought, and deed may falsely conclude that Calvinism promotes sinful behavior among believers. Likewise, the Calvinist who hears the Wesleyan speak of living a day without sin may falsely conclude that Wesleyanism simply redefines sin in terms of mistakes or shortcomings. Obviously, neither accurately represents the true theology or experience of the other.

Although unintentional sin is viewed quite differently than intentional sin, it is still taken very seriously in Wesleyan theology. All sin requires the atoning work of Christ. As Wesley put it; "Not only sin, properly so called (that is, a voluntary transgression of a known law), but sin, improperly so called (that is, an involuntary transgression of a divine law, known or unknown) needs the atoning blood."[10] The difference is that God's grace has already applied the atonement of Christ to our unintentional sins. That is why Wesleyans do not typically pray for forgiveness for unknown sins of word, thought, and deed. It is not that they believe themselves to be above the possibility of such sins, but that those sins are already forgiven. However,

---

[10]   *Works* 11:396.

it is thoroughly appropriate, and theologically consistent, for Wesleyans to offer prayers that acknowledge the reality of unintentional sin and to give thanks for God's endless mercy in covering those sins.

———•———

Wesley embraced a three-fold understanding of sin. In one sense, sin is understood as humanity's inherited state of rebellion against God. In a second sense, sin is defined as a willful violation of God's law. In a third sense, sin becomes more of a technical classification for the physical, mental, and emotional shortcomings that are inevitable consequences of fallen human nature existing in a fallen world.

The Wesleyan passion for authentic Christianity emerges from this sober awareness of the problem of sin. In spite of humanity's perfect beginning and holy state, sin was invited into the human experience. Wesleyanism recognizes the tragedy of the fall, the universal domination of sin, and the total corruption of the human race. For that reason, Wesleyanism is completely pessimistic about the fate of humanity in its fallen state. Wesleyanism becomes entirely optimistic, however, when it considers the gift of divine grace.

6

The Gift of Grace

Prevenient Grace

Augustine's Dilemma

THE COMPREHENSIVE domination of sin over humanity raises an important question. How can anyone be saved? If the fallen human race is so morally bankrupt that even calling out to God for help is beyond human ability, how is it that we are in fact able to do just that? The answer is God's grace. Grace refers to the gift of undeserved mercy extended by God to humanity. Both the Old and New Testaments are filled with references to and examples of God's grace. Every divine act of kindness, patience, and understanding is an act of grace. Although the concept was well known in the early church, it was Augustine who first gave it doctrinal structure.

According to Augustine, there are three main categories of grace. The first is prevenient grace. Prevenient comes from the Latin word for going ahead. Therefore, prevenient grace refers to God's first great act of mercy to humanity. It is God's initial work that prepares people for conversion. Since we cannot call out to him, he calls out to us. Furthermore, he enables us to hear his call and look his direction. This is the essence of prevenient grace. It is God's first step toward human redemption. The main emphasis is that God takes the initiative and is actively involved in the life of every person, even prior to their conversion.

Augustine's second category is operative grace, which is God's act of bestowing conversion upon a person. Augustine did not believe humanity had any role to play in salvation. Rather, he saw conversion as a divine decision and process that God confers on those he has chosen to save. Operative grace obviously implies a doctrine of predestination.

The third category in Augustine's system is cooperative grace. This is grace which does enter into partnership with humanity. It is the grace by

81

which God collaborates with the converted in developing their spiritual maturity. So while believers play no role in their conversion, they do participate in their spiritual growth.

Augustine believed grace was irresistible. That is, those upon whom God chose to grant his grace could not reject it. This does not mean, however, that God forces his grace on people. Rather, said Augustine, divine grace is so lovingly overwhelming that the recipient can not help but be persuaded by it. It is irresistible because it is so attractive and convincing.

There is another dimension of grace that could even be classed as a fourth category in Augustine's system. This is the grace of perseverance. Just as no one comes to salvation through their own effort, so also says Augustine, no one endures to the end through their own effort. Endurance is itself another irresistible gift of grace. True Christians persevere, not because God forces them to, but because the strength of God's grace guarantees that they will. So from beginning to end, Augustine can affirm that salvation is nothing but the work of God's grace. This was the foundation for much of the later thought on grace and predestination that was developed by Calvin and the Protestant reformers.

Wesley also placed great emphasis on the benefits of God's grace. However, he disagreed with Augustine's concept of operative grace and its inherent doctrine of predestination. Wesley could not accept this doctrine as scripturally valid, but he did see the theological dilemma that seemed to make predestination the only logical conclusion. The problem was rooted in the doctrine of total depravity. Augustine taught that the fall of Adam had reduced all of humanity to a mass of sin. The corruption was so thorough that there remained in humanity no ability whatsoever to step toward God. In fact, humans could not even be aware of God's existence. But if this were true, then how could Augustine explain the fact that some people actually do turn to God and are saved?

If the entire human race was lost in the fall, then it would stand to reason that the entire race would remain lost. On the other hand, if God chose to exercise his sovereignty over the power of evil by saving the human race, then it would stand to reason that all would be saved. What defies reason is for God to exercise his sovereignty over evil, and yet for that act to result in the salvation of only some rather than all. This was Augustine's dilemma. The only answer he saw possible was that those who are saved have been predestined for salvation by God. It was Augustine's way of affirming both humanity's depravity and God's sovereignty, while at the same time recognizing the fact that some people actually are saved. The doctrine of predestination, therefore, does not suddenly appear as an arbitrary decree from God. Rather, according to Augustine, it follows as a logical necessity from the doctrine of total depravity.

In fairness to Augustine, and later to Calvin and the reformers, it must be added that this doctrine was not based solely on a logical formula. Its proponents firmly believed the doctrine to be scripturally supported, especially in the book of Romans. Opponents of the doctrine, such as Arminius and Wesley, believed the doctrine's scriptural interpretations to be in error and theologically inconsistent.

Freedom to Choose

Several references have been made in this and other chapters to the distinctions between Calvinism and Arminianism. These two traditions represent the two major theological camps of Protestant Christianity. John Calvin (1509–64) lived in Geneva and was one of the great theologians of the Reformation. Building on much of the earlier thought of Augustine, he made profound contributions to the whole spectrum of Protestant theology. He is most remembered for his five points of predestination that are commonly illustrated by the acrostic **TULIP**: **T**otal depravity, **U**nconditional election, **L**imited atonement, **I**rresistible grace, and **P**erseverance of the saints. Predestination in Calvin's thought is:

> God's eternal decree, by which he compacted with himself what he willed to become of each man. For all are not created in equal condition; rather, eternal life is foreordained for some, eternal damnation for others. Therefore, as any man has been created to one or the other of these ends, we speak of him as predestined to life or to death.[1]

In contrast to the views of Calvin are those of James Arminius (1560–1609). Arminius was a Dutch theologian who taught at the University of Leiden. In most regards he was in agreement with Calvin. However, his point of disagreement was specifically on the matter of predestination. While the Bible does speak of predestination, Arminius believed Calvin had missed the biblical meaning. Rather than being a matter of God choosing who is saved and who is lost, Arminius believed the Bible to be teaching that God had predetermined that all who accept Christ will be saved and all who reject him will be lost. He did not believe individual souls were specifically predestined. Arminius defined predestination as "an eternal and gracious decree of God in Christ, by which he determines to justify and adopt believers, and to endow them with life eternal, but to condemn unbelievers, and impenitent

---

[1] *Calvin's Institutes*, abridged ed., ed. Donald K. McKim (Louisville: Westminster John Knox, 2001) 113 §3.21.5.

persons." He went on further to emphasis that predestination "is not that by which God resolves to save some particular persons . . . but to condemn others."[2]

Like Augustine and Calvin, Arminius believed in original sin and total depravity. He also accepted that in Adam's fall humanity had completely lost the capacity to choose righteousness. Freewill existed only to the extent of choosing among expressions of evil. In the state of original sin, "the freewill of man towards the true good is not only wounded, maimed, infirm, bent, and weakened; but it is also imprisoned, destroyed, and lost."[3] For Arminius, however, the freedom of human will was profoundly affected by prevenient grace. In this gift of divine mercy God restored to humanity the freedom to choose between good and evil.

It is at this point that many Calvinists believe Arminius denies the sovereignty of God. They protest that any human participation in the redemptive process rules out divine sovereignty because it makes people responsible for their own salvation. However, this view misses the crucial fact that the freedom to chose or reject God is itself a gift from God and an expression of his sovereignty. Arminianism firmly asserts that believers are absolutely powerless to contribute to their own salvation in any way. God is totally and utterly sovereign in all regards. This includes his sovereign decision to grant all people the freedom to either accept or reject the salvation that he offers.

Both the Arminian and the Calvinistic views of salvation begin and end with the sovereignty of God. The difference is in understanding how that sovereignty is expressed. The Arminian understanding is summarized in what he called the four divine decrees. The first decree was to appoint Christ as humanity's Redeemer. The second was to save those who would repent of their sin and believe on Jesus. The third was to extend prevenient grace to enable and help people to believe. The fourth was to save those who would believe and to condemn those who would not.

The consequence of these differing views of how God expresses his sovereignty is that Calvin and Arminius end up with differing views of the order of salvation. In Calvinism salvation begins with predestination and is then followed by regeneration (awakening the elect to God's irresistible call) and justification. In Arminianism salvation begins with prevenient grace (enabling all to hear God's universal call) and is then followed by justification and regeneration. Thus, not only is the beginning point completely different, but also the subsequent order. Whereas justification follows regeneration in

---

[2] *The Writings of James Arminius*, trans. James Nicholas and W. R. Bagnall (Grand Rapids: Baker, 1977) 2:470.
[3] Ibid., 1:526.

Calvin, justification precedes regeneration in Arminius. Furthermore, not only is the position of regeneration altered, but the concept itself is dissimilar.

Ten years after his death the views of Arminius were officially rejected at the Synod of Dort. Those convictions, however, did not vanish. They were embraced by those Protestants who sought an alternative to Calvin's view of predestination. Arminianism became popular in England and was widely accepted within the Church of England. Among Evangelicals, however, the term took on very negative connotations because it became associated with the humanistic element of the eighteenth century Enlightenment movement. Wesley reports that the reactions could be so severe, that "To say, 'This man is an Arminian,' has the same effect on many hearers, as to say, 'This is a mad dog.' It puts them into a fright at once: They run away from him with all speed and diligence; and will hardly stop, unless it be to throw a stone at the dreadful and mischievous animal."[4] For that reason Wesley did not commonly use the term prior to 1770.

Regardless of his effort to avoid the label, Wesley's Arminianism was obvious throughout his life and ministry. His 1740 sermon "Free Grace" outlined five specific objections to what he impolitely referred to as Calvinism's "horrible decree of predestination."[5]

First, he said, predestination negates the role of preaching. If eternal destinies are arbitrarily fixed by God, then there is no purpose in preaching. George Whitefield, as a Calvinist, argued that preaching still had merit in guiding people to better lives even if it did not have an evangelistic function. Wesley was not persuaded, for he saw conviction and conversion as the heart of preaching.

Second, predestination tends to discourage the pursuit of holiness. Wesley was quick to clarify that he did not mean Calvinists could not be holy. He only meant that the doctrine tended to diminish the value of holy qualities and character in the Christian's life.

Third, predestination tends to destroy Christian happiness. Here Wesley had in mind people who had accepted Christ, but still feared that they were among the reprobate who were predestined for hell. They believed in Jesus as Savior, but could not enjoy the comfort of that relationship.

Fourth, predestination tends to destroy the zeal for good works. Although Wesley did not believe good works contributed to salvation, he did believe them to be essential fruits of authentic faith that strengthen the believer.

---

[4] *Works* 10:358.
[5] *Works* 8:383.

Fifth, predestination contradicts the whole story of salvation as revealed in scripture. To Wesley, this doctrine made a mockery of the biblical account of God's grace and Christ's death.

Wesley adhered to the Arminian view that saw predestination as God's decree that all who believed would be saved. Election, on the other hand, had a somewhat different connotation. It was defined by Wesley as "a divine appointment of some particular men, to do some particular work in the world."[6] He looked to the appointments of Cyrus to rebuild the temple and Paul to preach the gospel as examples of election. Wesley was very clear that election had nothing to do with personal salvation. One could in fact be elected for a task or role and yet be eternally lost. Judas is the prime example of this. He was elected for apostleship, but in the end he chose a path that led to eternal condemnation.

This view of election also reveals Wesley's conviction that people can choose to move from belief to unbelief and thus forfeit their salvation. In other words, he rejected Augustine and Calvin's doctrine of perseverance of the saints, or eternal security. Wesleyans actually agree with Calvinists that no one can "lose" their salvation. In order for something to be lost it must accidentally pass out of possession. This cannot happen with salvation. However, salvation can be forfeited through conscious and deliberate abandonment of belief, though most Calvinists argue that such a person was never a true believer in the first place.

Pardon and Power

Wesley's understanding of prevenient grace centered on the two dimensions of forgiveness and enabling, or pardon and power. Like Augustine and Calvin, Wesley believed all humanity carries the guilt of Adam's sin, though he saw this guilt as more of a legal liability than personal blame. Regardless of that distinction, he believed this guilt was universally pardoned under God's prevenient grace. The reality and the consequences of human depravity still remained. The moral image of God was still lost. Human nature was still corrupted by an inherent spirit of rebellion against God and an instinctive impulse to do wrong, but the guilt itself was canceled.

This point must not be misunderstood. Wesleyan doctrine does not teach that people are born morally pure, or even morally neutral. All are born in a sinful state of total depravity. However, due to God's prevenient grace, all have been pardoned from the guilt of that inherited sin. The important meaning of this is that no one is condemned to eternal punishment prior to

---

6 *Works* 10:210.

their birth. Those who are eventually lost are lost solely as a result of their own acts of sin and their rejection of God's offer of redemption. Obviously, the Wesleyan view does not adhere to the doctrine of predestination as understood by Augustine and Calvin.

Wesleyanism further departs from Augustine and Calvin on the enabling aspect of prevenient grace. This divine empowerment partially restores the corrupted human faculties to the degree that people can sense their need of salvation and respond to God's offer. Wesley saw three particular aspects of human nature that were partially renewed. The first was *understanding*; specifically, the human capacity for grasping basic spiritual concepts. These include the existence of God and the difference between good and evil. The second was *liberty*. That is, the freedom to respond to God and the spiritual awareness that comes with understanding. The third was *volition*, or the will. Just having an intellectual awareness of God and the liberty to respond was not enough. The human will also needed a degree of restoration from depravity in order to make a choice for God an actual possibility.[7]

The Wesleyan view is the only one that takes into account the full impact of prevenient grace. Pelagius denied the reality of original sin and saw God's grace as merely enhancing the element of human understanding. Augustine denied the reality of human liberty and made God's grace a means of determining the human will. Wesleyan–Arminianism stands between these two positions and embraces the totality of God's work in a person.[8] Wesleyans understand that prevenient grace permeates the whole person by enlightening the understanding, activating liberty, and persuading the will. Through this grace God has restored humanity's fallen faculties to a level that allows all people to hear God's voice and look his direction.

Wesley recognized Augustine's theological dilemma, but he saw a different solution; one that affirms both human depravity and divine sovereignty but without imposing on God the moral problems of predestination. Whereas Augustine saw prevenient grace in a limited way, Wesley saw it universally. Augustine acknowledged that prevenient grace was extended in some measure to everyone. This was evident in the fact that even non-Christians have an awareness of God and some recognition of good and evil. But Augustine concluded that only the elect receive enough grace to awaken them to salvation, and that grace is irresistible. Wesley concluded that everyone receives sufficient grace to make a choice for or against God.

---

[7]   Randy L. Maddox, *Responsible Grace: John Wesley's Practical Theology* (Nashville: Kingswood, 1994) 87.

[8]   H. Orton Wiley, *Christian Theology* (Kansas City: Beacon Hill, 1952) 2:356.

Wesley and Pelagius

Many Wesleyans are surprised to discover that critics often associate Wesleyanism with Pelagianism—the heresy that denies the doctrine of original sin. Pelagius believed all human beings are born morally neutral. All enter life in the same moral state that Adam enjoyed in the beginning. Like Adam, all are perfectly capable of living a sinless life if they so choose. Therefore, salvation in Pelagianism is essentially a matter of the human will. Conversion is nothing more than one's own decision to accept God's truth and to live accordingly. There is no regeneration of the heart by the Holy Spirit, just a choice to live the right way.

So with the very obvious differences between Pelagianism and Wesleyanism, why do some critics allege that that there is a Pelagian strain in Arminian and Wesleyan doctrine? The charges usually have to do with the false notion that Wesleyans believe in salvation by works rather than grace. This misconception is usually fed by an inaccurate interpretation of the Wesleyan emphasis on prevenient grace, free will, good works, and Christian holiness. But Wesleyan theology is emphatically clear that God alone is the source of salvation and that salvation comes to us by grace alone. One of the first aspects of that grace is God's restoration of human free will so that people can respond to him. Since there is a response of faith toward God prior to salvation, there is obviously a type of divine-human cooperation, or synergism, at work in the salvation process. For those from a predestination mindset, any human participation in salvation, even though instituted by God, is Pelagianism.

It must be acknowledged, however, that some popular expressions of Wesleyanism do unintentionally have the look and sound of salvation by works. Wesley himself even made this mistake in his sometimes overly zealous efforts to distinguish Wesleyanism from Calvinism. Such stress was placed on Christian activity as to imply that these activities contribute to salvation. The emphasis on goods works almost seemed to overshadow the role of divine grace. Although this was never Wesley's actual position, he did come close to the point of Pelagianism in some regards. In fact, Wesleyan scholars openly acknowledge that Wesley can accurately be labeled as semi-Pelagian. That is, he was Pelagian in his insistence that people are free to exercise their own will in spiritual matters. However, he was thoroughly Augustinian in his insistence upon the sovereignty of God, the reality of original sin, and humanity's need for God's grace.

Wesley was by no means a Pelagian in the full sense of the word. It may be granted that he appeared to come close to it in some regards, but he also came equally close to Calvinism in other regards. He declared without apology that Wesleyans "may come to the very edge of Calvinism" on the following points: "(1) In ascribing all good to the free grace of God. (2) In denying all natural free-will, and all power antecedent to grace. And, (3) In excluding all merit from man; even for what good he has or does by the grace of God."[9] Yet through his understanding of prevenient grace, Wesley was able to find a middle ground between Augustinian–Calvinism and Pelagianism.

Wesley was, in fact, both semi-Augustinian and semi-Pelagian. And it was this remarkable doctrinal balance between divine grace and human responsibility that enabled him to speak to and for such a broad spectrum of evangelical Christianity. So squarely does Wesley fit within the mainstream of that movement that historian Mark Noll declared John and Charles Wesley to be the most effective advocates of the Reformation's basic message since the time of Martin Luther, John Calvin, Menno Simmons, and Thomas Cranmer. Noll describes the combined ministry of the Wesley brothers and George Whitefield as the single most important element in the transformation of the Reformation spirit into modern Protestant evangelicalism.[10]

Convincing Grace

The Dawning of Hope

As important as prevenient grace is in the system of Wesleyan doctrine, it is not the end. It is the beginning of the process by which God awakens the sinner to sin and its consequences. It takes convincing grace to bring the sinner to a point of repentance and conversion. Wesley affirmed this distinction in his sermon, "On Working Out Our Own Salvation," in which he said:

> salvation begins with what is usually termed (and very properly) 'preventing grace'; including the first wish to please God, the first dawn of light concerning his will, and the first, slight transient conviction of having sinned against him . . . . Salvation is carried on by 'convincing grace', usually in the scripture termed 'repentance.'[11]

Prevenient grace and convincing grace are not actually different types of grace, but rather different expressions of grace. All grace is the gift of unmerited love given to humanity by God. That love, however, is expressed in different ways according to the need. God's first act of love is to spiritually

---

[9]   *Works* 8:285.

[10]   Mark A. Noll, *Turning Points: Decisive Moments in the History of Christianity* (Grand Rapids: Baker, 1997) 223–24.

[11]   Albert C. Outler and Richard P. Heitzenrater, eds., *John Wesley's Sermons: An Anthology* (Nashville: Abingdon, 1991) 488.

awaken people and restore their capacity for response to him. Wesleyans call that expression of love prevenient grace. But then God intensifies the activity of the Holy Spirit more specifically by convincing, or convicting, individuals of their sinful condition. Prevenient grace alone does not accomplish this. It awakens people to God's presence, but it takes God's expression of convincing grace to awaken them to their sin.

Conviction is understood to be that work of the Holy Spirit which produces a sense of guilt and condemnation within sinners. Convincing grace stirs an awareness of personal guilt; not for Adam's sin, but for personal acts of sin. Furthermore, it brings the realization that guilt deserves punishment. However, the purpose of convincing grace is to produce hope, not hopelessness. For convincing grace always points to God's free gift of forgiveness and salvation in Christ. Thus, convincing grace is a double edged sword. Applied in one way it cuts through human arrogance to produce knowledge of guilt. Applied the other way it cuts through fear and condemnation to produce hope and trust.

The Unique Role of Preaching

Although convincing grace is the work of the Holy Spirit, it is a work that often utilizes human means. The Spirit convicts through the reading of scripture, prayer, the sacraments, life's circumstances, and conversations. The list of means is innumerable, but the primary means is preaching. This is most forcefully demonstrated in Romans 10:13-14: "Everyone who calls on the name of the Lord will be saved. How then can they call on the one they have not believed in? And how can they believe in the one of whom they have not heard? And how can they hear without someone preaching to them?"

Wesley was passionate about preaching. He would preach anywhere at anytime to anyone, often several times a day. The texts and subjects of his sermons varied, but they all had one primary aim: to be a means through which the Holy Spirit could convict of sin, call people to Christ, and strengthen the faithful. To the modern listener Wesley's sermons would be considered long, tedious, and academic. To the listeners of his day, however, they were powerful and culturally relevant with a heavy emphasis on application. After hearing others preach in Scotland, Wesley observed, "I heard many excellent truths . . . But as there was no application, it was likely to do as much good as the singing of a lark . . . no sinners are convinced of sin, none converted to God, by this way of preaching."[12] Although Wesley's preaching was intended to be intensely practical, his first priority was that it be biblically based and

---

[12]   *Works* 4:155.

Christ centered. A. Skevington Wood concluded that Wesley's preaching was so effective primarily because he was not ashamed to be known first and foremost as a preacher of the Bible.[13]

Despite the common image of Wesley preaching to great crowds, that does not accurately depict the full picture. In fact, preaching in the Wesleyan tradition was also about small gatherings and informal conversations. Much of Wesley's preaching was spontaneous. When arriving at an inn for an overnight stop he was often known to gather the guests together for a sermon and prayers. Likewise, he was constantly about the business of "preaching" while riding in a coach or walking the countryside. Wesley preached, in one sense or another, whenever and wherever he met people. This fact has caused Oxford scholar John Walsh to conclude that the most characteristic image of Wesley's impact in England is not of him preaching to vast crowds, but of him explaining the love of God to small groups in informal settings.[14] It is through the medium of preaching, in whatever environment and form, that the Holy Spirit most often and most effectively communicates the gift of God's grace.

Wesleyanism shares a common point of beginning with Calvin and the reformers in the doctrines of divine sovereignty and human depravity. However, their differing understandings of grace set their respective theologies on separate paths. It is the Wesleyan concept of prevenient grace that allows it to embrace without contradiction the four fundamental themes of total depravity, salvation by grace, human response, and the offer of salvation for all. Calvinism can hold only the first two themes, with the later two being replaced by the doctrines of predestination and election.[15]

The Wesleyan view of authentic faith is utterly dependent upon God's grace. It affirms, along with all of historic Christianity, that humanity is hopelessly lost in sin apart from grace. We are absolutely powerless to save ourselves in any way. But Wesleyan doctrine also affirms that through the gift of prevenient grace God awakens us to his presence and enables us to respond. In his sovereignty he renews our free will and initiates a divine-human cooperation. And finally, Wesleyanism affirms the role of the Holy Spirit in

---

[13]   A. Skevington Wood, *The Burning Heart: John Wesley, Evangelist* (Grand Rapids: Eerdmans, 1967) 209.

[14]   John Walsh, "Methodism and the Origins of English-Speaking Evangelicalism," in *Evangelicalism: Comparative Studies of Popular Protestantism in North America, the British Isles, and Beyond, 1700–1990,* ed. Mark A. Noll, David W. Bebbington, and George A. Rawlyk (Oxford: Oxford University Press, 1994) 34.

[15]   Collins, *Scripture Way of Salvation,* 45.

convicting us of sin and pointing us to the Savior. All of this is God's free gift to lost humanity.

7

The Offer of Redemption

The Person and Work of Christ

Who Jesus Is

THE TRANSFORMATION from sin to salvation is made possible by the grace of God, but it is actually accomplished through the person of Jesus. Wesleyans stand resolutely with historic Christianity in affirming both the full divinity and the full humanity of Jesus. He is the Son of God, the second person of the divine Trinity. As this statement implies, Wesleyans adhere to the traditional doctrine of the Trinity—Father, Son, and Holy Spirit. Wesley said, "I do not see how it is possible for any to have vital religion who denies that the Three are One."[1] The Wesleyan belief in the divinity of Jesus is balanced with a corresponding belief in the full humanity of Jesus. He is God in the flesh who was born of the Virgin Mary in order to redeem lost humanity. In this, Wesleyans affirm their allegiance to the traditional doctrine of the Incarnation.

The first major theological debate to emerge in the early church centered on Christology; that is, the doctrine of Christ. This debate gave rise to several heresies that were eventually rejected by the church. While some erred by overstressing the humanity of Jesus, others overstressed his divinity. Two of the most prominent heresies were Docetism and Arianism

Docetism denied the humanity of Jesus. Its name comes from a Greek word meaning "to seem." Docetism taught that Jesus was a purely divine being who only seemed to be human. This view was linked to a philosophy known as Gnosticism. The Gnostics believed that all physical matter, including the entire created universe, is evil. Since the human body is made of physical matter, the body itself is evil. The Gnostics accepted the divinity of

---

[1] *Works* 6:205.

Jesus, but with their flawed concept of the physical world they could not accept that he was human. If Jesus was actually human, then he would have to possess a human body, and therefore, he himself would be evil. So Gnostics taught the Docetic view that Jesus was not actually born in a human body. Rather, he was a spirit who was poured through the body of Mary, thus giving the illusion of physical birth.

This heresy carried serious doctrinal dangers for the early church; for just as it denied the physical birth of Jesus, so it also denied the physical death and resurrection of Jesus. Thus, the entire New Testament teaching on the person and work of Jesus as we know it was dismissed. This heresy was already well known within the lifetime of the apostles. The writings of Paul and John contain direct rebuttals to it. The most obvious of which is in 1 John 1:1-3, where John gives a specific eyewitness testimony to the fact that Jesus was a real person with a real human body.

Arianism was a heresy that rose to prominence early in the third century. Its founder, Arius, began teaching that Jesus was neither human nor divine. He was, rather, a different type of being altogether. He was God's first and greatest creation, standing between divinity and humanity. He was of a similar substance to God, but not the same substance as God. The theologian Athanasius led the fight against Arianism and it was officially condemned. However, it became widely accepted in spite of official rejection and remained a subject of debate for several centuries.

These and other heretical views on the person of Christ were eventually dismissed and the church settled on what remains the accepted understanding of Christology. Christ is one person with two complete natures; a single person who is fully human as well as fully divine. His unity with the Father is absolute in all regards, including essence, substance, nature, and glory. Wesley saw no reason to add to or take from that traditional statement of faith. He was solidly committed to the accepted doctrine of Christ. He did tend, however, to give greater emphasis to the divinity of Jesus over his humanity. He held firmly to the orthodox creeds of the church and prayed that those associated with his ministry would "be saved from supposed 'improvements' upon the apostolic testimony or presumed Christological innovations."[2]

What Jesus Has Done

Having arrived at a general point of consensus on who Jesus is, the church next had to think though the question of what Jesus has actually done. Perhaps the most comprehensive answer to that question is simply to say that

---

[2] Thomas C. Oden, *John Wesley's Scriptural Christianity: A Plain Exposition of His Teachings on Christian Doctrine* (Grand Rapids: Zondervan, 1994) 177.

he has atoned for the sin of the world. To make atonement literally means to cover something over. So Christ's work of atonement through his crucifixion and resurrection is his work of covering over our sin. On this point all Christians generally agree. However, understanding the exact sense in which Christ's atonement is applied to our sin is another matter. Numerous theories of atonement have emerged over the centuries. Three theories in particular have been most widely accepted. They all affirm that Jesus is our atonement, but they reflect different ideas of how his act of atonement is applied to the problem of sin.

The *Ransom Theory* is based on several scripture passages that refer to Christ as the ransom for our sin (Matthew 20:28; Mark 10:45; 1 Timothy 2:6; Hebrews 9:15). This theory sees sinful humanity as having fallen captive to Satan. We are hopelessly bound and enslaved by him. The sacrificial death of Christ, however, has paid the ransom price to Satan for our release. This view seems to have reasonable support from both scripture and human experience. Sin does indeed enslave, as the theory says. The main objection to the theory is its image of Satan somehow demanding a ransom payment from God. Satan holds no power over God and is in no position to dictate terms of negotiation.

The *Moral Influence Theory* takes an entirely different approach. It sees Christ's death not as payment, but as the ultimate example of God's love. His death atones for sin only in the sense of convincing people of God's love for them. This realization then inspires them to turn away from sin and toward God. This view is compatible with the Pelagianism denial of original sin and belief in humanity's ability to simply choose to turn to God. It is also very acceptable to modern liberalism's assumptions on the goodness of human nature. However, this theory is not generally accepted by those who take seriously the doctrines of original sin and total depravity.

The *Satisfaction Theory* sees humanity as being in debt to God due to sin. We owe back to him a debt of righteousness because our sin violates and dishonors his holiness. But there is a twofold dilemma. On the one hand, we are utterly incapable of paying this debt. On the other hand, God cannot simply cancel the debt because such light treatment of sin would itself be a further act of dishonor against his holiness. Thus God would be in the unthinkable position of dishonoring himself. His solution was to send his Son to die as the only acceptable substitute payment for the debt we owe. In this way, God has not merely dismissed the debt, but has paid it himself on our behalf. In this act God has preserved his own honor, integrity, and holiness, while at the same time making possible our salvation. This was the theory favored by Wesley.

John Calvin developed an alternate version of the satisfaction theory called the punishment (or penal) theory. Its basic premise is essentially the same, but with a different outlook on the nature of sin's violation. Whereas the satisfaction theory views sin as the dishonoring of God's holiness, the punishment theory sees it as the breaking of God's law. Therefore, sin does not represent a debt to be paid, but an offense to be punished. God's justice has been violated and the penalty is death. So Christ's crucifixion is not a substitute payment, but a substitute punishment.

A second alternate version of the satisfaction theory is the governmental theory, which was developed by a student of James Arminius named Hugo Grotius. According to this view, it is not God's honor or justice that seeks satisfaction, but his moral character. Grotius saw God as the Moral Governor of the universe. In order for God's governing authority to remain intact, he had to send his Son to suffer for humanity's sin. This suffering was neither ransom nor punishment. It was the upholding of God's moral authority. The distinction between suffering and punishment is significant. Punishment implies guilt, but suffering does not. Therefore, since Jesus bore no guilt for our sin, his suffering was not a form of punishment.

Wesleyans can be found across the full spectrum of atonement theories, with the general exception of the moral influence theory. While Wesley was most at ease with the satisfaction theory, he frequently used the language of the punishment theory and was sympathetic to some aspects of the governmental theory.

The Scope of Salvation

The study of Christ's redemptive work not only forces an examination of the person of Christ and the nature of atonement, but also the scope of salvation. In other words, it raises the question of who reaps the eternal benefit of Christ's work. That is, who will be saved in the end? There are three options: everyone will be saved; only the elect will be saved; or only the believers will be saved.

The first option, universalism, is the belief that ultimately everyone will be saved. This may be accomplished either through God's general forgiveness of all sin, or through some final means of persuasion that brings all to accept Christ. Universalism must not be confused with God's universal offer of salvation. Wesleyans believe God has provided for the salvation of all and that he offers salvation to all. However, they reject any doctrine that claims guaranteed salvation for all. Wesley saw universalism as a spiritual sedative that keeps sinners content in their sin and soothes the awakened back into apathy. In a letter to William Law he wrote; "There can hardly be any doctrine under heaven more agreeable to flesh and blood; nor any which more directly tends to prevent the very dawn of conviction. . . . None more naturally tends to keep men asleep in sin, and to lull asleep those who begin to be awakened."[3]

The second option, election, has already been discussed in the previous chapter. It is the belief that salvation is only for those whom God has predestined to receive it. According to this teaching, the atonement of Christ applies only to the elect. Wesleyans have always rejected this limited view of God's grace and Christ's work.

Wesleyanism teaches the third option. This is the belief that salvation is universally offered through Christ, but is only received by those who choose to believe and accept God's offer. Through prevenient grace, God awakens people to their need and enables them to respond to him for salvation. Salvation is neither limited to the elect nor guaranteed for all. Rather, it is a gift to be received by any who respond in faith to Christ.

First Steps toward Salvation

Repentance: Turning from Sin

Salvation is offered freely to all, but it is only received by those who accept it. This means God's offer demands a response. This response has two essential components: repentance and faith. To repent means to turn away from sin with intent to follow God. The theme of repentance as a prerequisite to salvation is recurrent throughout the Bible. Perhaps Peter stated it most succinctly in Acts 3:19, "Repent, then, and turn to God, so that your sins may be wiped out, that times of refreshing may come from the Lord." Repentance is far more than mere apology, or even an expression of regret. Regret is a part of repentance, but it is not the same thing. Regret has to do with consequences. We regret doing something because we realize it has produced negative results. We may even wish to make amends for our wrong action. But repentance is quite different. It has to do with actually being disgusted by sin itself and making a radical break from it. It begins as an acknowledgement of sin, which is then followed by a genuine sense of sorrow over sin, and culminates in a conscious determination to turn away from sin.

Repentance can be seen in terms of a three stage process: conviction, shame, and change. The concept of convicting grace was discussed in the previous chapter. This is the work of the Holy Spirit that not only makes individuals aware of their sin, but actually makes them uncomfortable with that

---

[3]   *Works* 9:501.

sin. They see sin for what it is and themselves for what they are. Conviction is that act of grace by which the Spirit causes people to be repulsed by their sin. It is the first stage of repentance.

Remorse, or shame, follows quickly after conviction. Job and Ezra are two biblical characters who expressed the essence of remorse. Job declared, "My ears had heard of you but now my eyes have seen you. Therefore I despise myself and repent in dust and ashes" (42:5-6). Ezra expressed remorse on behalf of his people when he prayed, "O my God, I am too ashamed and disgraced to lift up my face to you, my God, because our sins are higher than our heads and our guilt has reached to the heavens" (9:5-6). Shame and remorse may be profound and sincere, but they are not the same as repentance. Judas experienced great remorse over his betrayal of Jesus, but he did not repent.

True repentance does not occur until conviction and remorse result in change. This change is not merely self-improvement. It is, rather, a radical turn toward an entirely new orientation. It is breaking from sin with a determined resolve to obey and serve God. Repentance is a direct result of God's prevenient grace that awakens people to their sin and enables them to respond. In no sense can it be said that repentance is a human initiative. It is a human response to God's initiative that is made possible only by his grace.

Although repentance and faith are not identical, they are interrelated. Two points are to be made here. First, Wesley believed repentance precedes faith and is necessary to it: "Repentance absolutely must go before faith."[4] Second, he believed repentance is necessary to salvation, but not in the same way as faith. He was clear that we are saved through faith, not repentance: "Faith is the sole condition of this salvation."[5] However, repentance is necessary to salvation in the sense that it "is a sign of our readiness to receive the further gifts of God."[6] It is also necessary to the degree that it is the forerunner of justifying faith. So while Wesleyans would never say salvation comes from repentance, they do say repentance prepares the way for the faith that does result in salvation. In this way it is affirmed that repentance is a necessary prerequisite to salvation, but it is not the means of salvation.

Faith: Turning to God

Faith is one of the most used words in Christianity. It is also one of the most ambiguous words. It can carry many different shades of meaning accord-

---

[4] Works 8:47.

[5] Ibid.

[6] Kenneth J. Collins, The Scripture Way of Salvation: The Heart of John Wesley's Theology (Nashville: Abingdon, 1997) 66.

ing to its context. It can refer to a very broad category of doctrine, as in the Christian faith. It can also imply belief, confidence, reliance, expectation, or even encouragement. Throughout the Bible, the prevailing theme that unifies the understanding of faith is the theme of trust. Unfortunately, faith is often thought of in a very incomplete way that reduces it to nothing more than wishful thinking or blind acceptance of what cannot be explained. Even worse, it is sometimes equated with ignorance or actions that are contrary to common reason. Although faith may occasionally include some of these things as part of an overall change of heart and mind, none of these represents the true meaning of faith.

Faith actually does involve knowledge and reason. It begins with evidence. Saving faith begins with the evidence of sin and the evidence of God's provision. This knowledge is not acquired solely by human means. Much of it is evidence of the heart that is revealed by God through the convicting work of the Holy Spirit. Other aspects, however, do come through human means; such as preaching and witnessing. Although salvation is not based on knowledge, it is very difficult to conceive of anyone coming to saving faith without at least some minimal knowledge of the gospel. But awareness of sin and knowledge of Christ do not in themselves lead to repentance and faith.

In order for faith to progress from knowledge to persuasion, it must also involve the element of belief. As Wesley noted in his sermon, "Salvation by Faith," even devils have knowledge of sin, Christ, and redemption; but that does not mean they have saving faith. Saving faith begins with awareness of sin, but then moves to belief in both the need for salvation and the provision of Christ.

Faith culminates in trust. Saving faith is realized when we cast ourselves into God's grace and trust Christ for the salvation that he offers. This is the natural consequence of true belief. This is God's gift of faith.

Wesley's understanding of faith took several years to develop as he progressed on his spiritual journey. As a young man at Oxford he saw faith purely in terms of reason and intellectual assent. But under Peter Bohler's influence he came to see that faith is much more than mere assent. He came to agree with Bohler's definition that faith is "A sure trust and confidence which a man hath in God, that through the merits of Christ *his* sins are forgiven, and *he* reconciled to the favour of God."[7]

Shortly after making the above notation on the nature of faith, Wesley experienced his Aldersgate conversion. One month later, he preached his "Salvation by Faith" sermon before Oxford University in St. Mary's Church. He clearly distinguished between faith as a general awareness of God, or

---

7   *Works* 1:90.

even an intellectual knowledge of the gospel, and faith as trust in Christ. He spoke of three kinds of faith that are not saving faith. First, is what he called the faith a heathen. That is, a vague belief in the existence of a divine being. Second, is the faith of a devil. This refers to those who know who Jesus is and what the Bible says, but do not love God. Third, is the faith of the apostles. Since the apostles had the unique benefit of physically seeing and knowing Jesus in a way that subsequent believers have not, Wesley did not consider their faith to be the same as what we call saving faith.

Wesley's strong affirmation in this sermon was that "Christian faith is then, not only an assent to the whole of the gospel of Christ, but also a full reliance on the blood of Christ; a trust in the merits of his life, death and resurrection."[8] Once Wesley reached this point of understanding he remained adamant for the rest of his life that faith was essentially a matter of trust, although it did also contain a degree of intellectual assent.

Wesley also recognized that faith cannot be acquired by human effort. It is a gift from God. This gift, however, does not come fully developed. Rather, it comes as a seed that must be nurtured. Thus, believers experience stages and levels of faith as they grow in grace. Christians do not create their own faith, but they do exercise their faith in order for it to strengthen and mature.

Finally, as important as faith is in the process of salvation, it is not the actual cause of salvation. The specific biblical concept of justification by faith was rediscovered and propagated by Martin Luther and the Reformers in the sixteenth century. Contrary to some popular misconceptions, justification by faith does not mean we are saved because of, or on account of, our faith. That would make faith itself the savior. Rather, we are saved when by faith we receive God's offer of salvation that is made possible through Jesus. It is most accurate to say that we are justified *by* grace *through* faith.

The redemptive work of Christ is accomplished through his atoning death and resurrection. As the Son of God, fully divine and fully human, he alone could stand in our place to bear the cost of our sin. He has provided the way for all to be reunited with God in a fresh and pure relationship. The only thing lacking is the response of individuals to this offer of redemption. It is a response that begins with sincere repentance and is completed with trusting faith. This is the Wesleyan view of the beginning of the authentic Christian life that is to follow.

---

[8] *Works* 5:9.

8

The Transformation of New Birth

What Happens to the Believer

Justification: A Dramatic Acquittal

THE TREATMENT of several key theological terms is necessary in order to describe what actually happens to a person at conversion. Conversion itself carries a similar meaning to repentance. It has to do with being set in a new direction. It is the word generally used in reference to the act of becoming a Christian. But conversion involves a number of components that contribute to the overall life-changing character of this experience. These components can be identified individually for the sake of doctrinal discussion, but in the actual experience of coming to know Christ as Savior they are tightly interwoven. One does not exist apart from the others, nor are they necessarily separated by a sequence of time. In other words, these are all different works that God does in the single moment when saving faith is exercised and a person is converted to Christ.

Justification is one of the dominant themes in the writings of Paul. He uses the word justification (or justify) some thirty times. It is essentially a legal term that carries the idea of God's acquittal, or forgiveness, of sin. God is the Judge; sinners are the guilty offenders. Those who repent are declared not guilty by God. This is not a mere dismissal of the charges, but a full pardon. The difference is significant. A guilty person who has his charges dismissed is still guilty. In spite of his guilt the authorities decide, usually for some technical reason, not to pursue the case and inflict the deserved penalty. The offender has literally gotten away with his crime. An acquittal, however, is a full release from guilt for one who has already been found guilty and is awaiting punishment. This is what happens when a sinner is justified by God. There is forgiveness of sin, acquittal of guilt, and acceptance into the favor of God.

Closely associated with the biblical idea of justification are the concepts of forgiveness and righteousness. To be justified is to be forgiven. The language of forgiveness is commonly used in evangelistic appeals because it is more readily understood than the more technical language of justification. The meaning, however, is essentially the same. To forgive someone is not the same as overlooking, ignoring, or passively accepting their offense. Forgiveness means acquittal or pardon; it is the releasing of guilt. This distinction between releasing guilt and overlooking guilt is subtle but crucial. Guilt that is overlooked has no restorative quality. Its presence remains painfully obvious to others even though they pretend it is not there. Beneath the surface of the relationship lurk mistrust, suspicion, and resentment.

True forgiveness is restorative. It embodies trust and acceptance. The future relationship is unaffected by the past offense. Wesley emphasized this understanding when he said, "The plain scriptural notion of justification is pardon, the forgiveness of sins. . . . His sins, all his past sins, in thought, word, and deed, are covered, are blotted out, shall not be remembered or mentioned against him, any more than if they had not been."[1] This statement not only reveals Wesley's definition of justification, it also reveals his insistence that forgiveness is extended only to past sins, not future sins. Willful, deliberate sins committed after justification will need to be confessed and forgiven at that time.

The Christian concept of divine forgiveness is unknown in other religions. They may incorporate rituals of appeasement for their divinities, but this too is quite different from forgiveness. Appeasement is based on bargaining. A deal is agreed as to what type of payment must be made to avert divine wrath; the greater the offense, the greater the appeasement price. This is not forgiveness. God's forgiveness flows from his holiness and love. Humanity is utterly incapable of offering a payment high enough to appease for sin. But God, out of pure love, paid the price himself on the cross and freely extended complete forgiveness to all who would accept it. Through Christ the just demands of God's holy law have been fully satisfied and the repentant sinner is, therefore, justified by God's grace.

Righteousness is the other concept closely tied to justification. The two words actually come from the same Greek root. Righteousness has to do with right character and conduct. The popular connotation of the term often focuses solely on conduct, thus conjuring up images of rigid Puritans or reclusive monks. True righteousness does involve right behavior, but it is behavior that flows from right character. To be righteous in the biblical sense means the same as being justified; that is, to be approved or accepted by God.

---

[1] *Works* 5:57.

The theme of righteousness carries within it a subtle, but important, question. When Paul states in Romans 5:1 that "we have been justified through faith," he is saying that all true believers are now righteous. But in what sense are they righteous? Does he mean they have merely been declared righteous, or does he mean they have actually been made righteous? That is, does God merely view the forgiven sinner as righteous for Christ's sake, or does God actually make the forgiven sinner righteous? Imputed righteousness (God views the sinner as righteous) and imparted righteousness (God makes the sinner righteous) are the theological terms used to refer to these two ideas.

Based on the thought of Luther and Calvin, the reformers taught that God does not make sinners righteous, but only accepts Christ's righteousness in place of their missing righteousness. The sinner's guilt was placed on Christ on the cross; in exchange, the righteousness of Christ was placed on the sinner. Therefore, God considers the sinner to be righteous, even though he actually is not. In this way God can view the sinner as meriting salvation because the sinner clings to the righteousness of Christ. This is the doctrine of imputed righteousness.

Wesley disagreed with the reformers understanding of this doctrine: "Least of all does justification imply, that God is deceived in those whom he justifies; that he thinks them to be what, in fact, they are not; that he accounts them to be otherwise than they are."[2] Wesley had a different understanding of why God can view the justified sinner as righteous. It is not because the righteousness of Christ has been placed over the new Christian, but because God gives the believer a righteousness that truly is the believer's own. That is, he actually makes the believer righteous through the cleansing work of the Holy Spirit. This is the doctrine of imparted righteousness.

Reconciliation: Bridging the Gap

Conversion also means reconciliation in that "we were reconciled to him through the death of his Son" (Romans 5:10). Obviously, the fact that believers are now reconciled to God through Christ indicates that they were previously separated from God. This alienation, as discussed earlier, is a direct consequence of sin. But through the atonement of Christ people are called to cease their hostility toward their Creator and be reunited with him. Many theologians regard the theme of reconciliation as the central feature of the entire salvation story. Paul deals with this theme extensively and at three

---

[2] Ibid.

different levels: reconciliation between God and humanity; reconciliation between one human being and other; and reconciliation of all creation.[3]

First, reconciliation is personal—individuals are reconciled to God. In the words of scripture; "we were reconciled to him through the death of his Son . . . we also rejoice in God through our Lord Jesus Christ through whom we have now received reconciliation" (Romans 5:10-11). It is in his letter to the Colossians that Paul states this amazing truth best, "Once you were alienated from God and were enemies in your minds because of your evil behavior. But now he has reconciled you by Christ's physical body through death to present you holy in his sight, without blemish and free from accusation" (1:21-22). These and other verses like them make three things very clear: sin is the cause of humanity's separation from God; Christ's atoning death is the solution to that separation; and it is we who are reconciled to God rather than God being reconciled to us. The last distinction is important. God came to us where we were in our sin. However, he did not come to reconcile himself to us, but to make the way possible for us to be reconciled to him. God is not the one in need of reconciliation; we are. He did not sin against us; we sinned against him.

Second, reconciliation is social—individuals are reconciled to each other. Salvation is not a purely private matter. It is not just about our own personal relationship with God, it is also about those around us and our relationship with them. Paul's emphasis in Ephesians on the unity of believers and John's calls for mutual love speak to this. In the New Testament church the factions of division were often along Jewish-Gentile lines. Each group came to Christ from very different backgrounds. This was at the core of the first tensions and debates of the church. Other differences developed as some people began to identify themselves as supporters of certain of traveling evangelists rather than as followers of Jesus. These divisions threatened to destroy the early church. But the reconciling power of Christ is not limited only to problems between believers. All interpersonal reconciliation is rooted in the atoning work of Christ. Individuals, groups, and even nations are able to be united in peace through God's provision for reconciliation.

Third, reconciliation is cosmic—the entire created order is reconciled to God. The presence of sin and evil has not only affected the human race; it has affected all of creation. Romans 8:19-21 speaks of the entire universe awaiting the final glory of renewal that will one day come. That is why Paul is able to declare that "God was pleased to have all his fullness dwell in him, and through him to reconcile to himself all things, whether things on earth

---

[3]   H. Ray Dunning, *Grace, Faith, and Holiness: A Wesleyan Systematic Theology* (Kansas City: Beacon Hill, 1988) 341.

or things in heaven, by making peace through his blood shed on the cross" (Colossians 1:19-20). This reconciliation of all things cannot be taken as support for a doctrine of universal salvation for all people. It is, rather, an indication of the grand cosmic scale to which God's work of reconciliation is extended.

It is apparent, however, that all of these things have not yet actually happened. People still rebel against God, marriages still end in divorce, nations still go to war, and the universe still awaits its re-creation. Although reconciliation is available here and now through Christ, it is not yet fulfilled in the sense that God ultimately has in mind. That final reconciliation is still to come. But that future aspect does not detract from the present power and reality of what is now available to all who believe in the atoning work of Christ. He offers reconciliation to all, but not all accept the offer. Thus Paul pleaded with the Corinthians, "We implore you on Christ's behalf: Be reconciled to God" (2 Corinthians 5:20).

Adoption: Welcome to the Family

The concept of adoption continues the theme of reconciliation and takes it a step further. Not only are believers reconciled to become friends with God, they are actually adopted as his children. Specifically, the idea carried forth is that believers are allowed to share in the benefits of Christ's own Sonship to the Father. Adopted as children of God, believers have "received the Spirit of sonship. And by him we cry, 'Abba, Father'" (Romans 8:15). The primary purpose of adoption in ancient Greek and Roman culture was inheritance. A man adopted a son if he wanted that person to have his inheritance. This too is the primary purpose of God's adopting grace. He wants all who will believe to share with Christ the inheritance that is to come. As Paul goes on to explain, "Now if we are children, then we are heirs—heirs of God and co-heirs with Christ" (Romans 8:17).

In his sermon "The Spirit of Bondage and Adoption," Wesley emphasized the sharp contrast between the former life of bondage and the new life of adoption. In that moment of reconciliation and adoption several old things come to an end.

> Here end both the guilt and the power of sin. . . . Here end remorse, and sorrow of heart, and the anguish of wounded spirit. . . . Here ends also that bondage unto fear. . . . He cannot fear any longer the wrath of God; for he knows it is now turned away from him, and looks upon Him no longer as an angry Judge, but as a loving Father. He cannot fear the devil, knowing he has no power. . . . He fears not

hell; being an heir of the kingdom of heaven: Consequently, he has no fear of death.[4]

In exchange for the bondage of fear that dominated his old life, the believer receives the liberating freedom of adoption. This is "liberty not only from guilt and fear, but from sin, from that heaviest of all yokes, that basest of all bondage. His labour is not now in vain. The snare is broken, and he is delivered. He not only strives, but likewise prevails; he not only fights, but conquers also."[5] The imagery is reminiscent of the famous third verse in Charles Wesley's hymn "And Can It Be":

> Long my imprisoned spirit lay,
> Fast bound in sin and nature's night.
>
> Thine eye diffused a quickening ray.
> I woke; the dungeon flamed with light!
>
> My chains fell off, my heart was free;
> I rose, went forth, and followed thee.

But for John Wesley, the prominent characteristic of reconciliation and adoption is love. Not just God's love for us, but our love in return to him. Wesley viewed humanity in three states: the natural state, the legal state, and the evangelical state. The natural state refers to those who live with no regard to God. They may hate him or they may ignore him. Either way they live unto themselves apart from him. The legal state refers to those who have been awakened to God and their need of him. They realize that they are under God's law. They may even try to do right and live for him within their own strength, but they have not thrown themselves onto his mercy and grace for forgiveness. The evangelical state refers to those who have done so, and now belong to Christ in the full sense. Wesley's point is this: "the *natural* man neither fears nor loves God; one *under the law*, fears; one *under grace*, loves him."[6] He sometimes referred to those in the legal state as having the faith of a servant, while those in the state of grace had the faith of a son. This is the essence of adoption; moving by faith in Christ from the state of a fearful servant to the state of a loved and loving son or daughter.

---

[4] *Works* 5:106–7.
[5] Ibid., 107.
[6] Ibid, 108.

What Happens in the Believer

Regeneration: A Fresh Start

The overall experience of conversion is both objective and subjective. That is, it involves those things just discussed that God does for us, but it also involves certain things he does within us. The first of these is regeneration. Regeneration is most simply defined as the New Birth. This is the fundamental transformation of life that God brings about in the new believer. It is the renewal of the person's spiritual life that makes possible continuing faith, love, obedience, and growth. For some this will be expressed in a radical shift of lifestyle and behavior. For others the outward expression may be more subtle. But regardless of variations in outward expression, the inward transformation in all cases is identical. When a repentant sinner exercises saving faith in Christ, that person is reborn into a new life in Christ. "Therefore," Paul writes, "if anyone is in Christ, he is a new creation; the old has gone, the new has come!" (2 Corinthians 5:17).

Jesus first introduced the idea of regeneration in his famous nighttime conversation with Nicodemus. He shocked the educated Pharisee with the puzzling declaration; "You must be born again" (John 3:7). Jesus then went on to acknowledge that the exact nature of this rebirth is a mystery to the human mind. He likened it to the wind, which "blows wherever it pleases. You hear its sound, but you cannot tell where it comes from or where it is going. So it is with everyone born of the Spirit" (John 3:8). The imagery of rebirth is readily understood. It signifies a new beginning, a fresh start, a new life, a new family, new values, and a new future. Exactly how God does this, however, is not readily understood. According to Jesus, the nature and means of this transformation is so profound that it simply transcends human reason. For the people of the ancient world Jesus put it in terms of the wind; they could see its effects, but they could not understand its nature.

Although regeneration is inseparable from justification, they are not the same thing. Justification speaks of the relative change that comes with conversion. That is, the new believer has gone from being an enemy against God to being a child of God. There has been a radical change in his standing before God. Regeneration speaks not of this outward relative change, but of an actual inner change. It speaks of the fundamental change of heart that gives new life. Believers are not just viewed by God as being different, they actually are different. Obviously, the concept of regeneration is closely linked to the doctrine of imparted righteousness.

The doctrine of regeneration marks yet another distinction between Calvinists and Wesleyans. Calvin believed regeneration precedes repentance.

That is, no one can repent and believe until they have first been reborn. So for Calvin, regeneration is God's way of awakening the elect to their salvation. Once reborn in spirit, they see God's plan of salvation and are irresistibly drawn to repentance and faith.

Wesley, like Arminius before him, saw that regeneration follows repentance and faith rather than preceding them. The New Birth is not the cause of repentance, but one of the results of repentance. No one is reborn in spirit until they have first responded to God's prevenient grace by repenting and believing. The Wesleyan objection to Calvin is that he seemed to confuse regeneration with prevenient grace. The Calvinistic objection to Arminius and Wesley was their insistence that human beings actually do have a cooperative role to play in their own salvation.

Another view of regeneration held in some Baptist and Anabaptist traditions is that it occurs simultaneously with the act of baptism. This is the doctrine of baptismal regeneration. The idea is based on scripture verses such as Titus 3:5; "He saved us through the washing of rebirth and renewal by the Holy Spirit." In its most extreme form it teaches that even if one repents and believes, yet dies before being baptized, he will be denied entrance into heaven.

Baptismal regeneration has traditionally been rejected by both Wesleyans and most Calvinists. Wesley himself, however, took a position that has left him vulnerable to misinterpretation on both sides. Some have maintained that he staunchly rejected the doctrine. Others have said he enthusiastically embraced it. Still others have claimed he was hopelessly inconsistent. There are good reasons for this diversity of interpretations of Wesley's position. In his *Treatise on Baptism* he clearly supports the concept of baptismal regeneration. But in his sermon "The New Birth" he is equally clear in supporting regeneration apart from baptism. He places it, instead, squarely within the context of the conversion experience. The eminent Wesley scholar Albert Outler concluded that Wesley tolerated a "mild allowance of the doctrine of baptismal regeneration."[7] Therefore, it can be said that he believed in regeneration in both senses.

Wesley's actual position was that true regeneration could, and sometimes did, occur at baptism, but it was not necessarily linked to baptism. He believed there were those who were born again prior to baptism, and there were those who were baptized without being born again. But he also believed many sincere seekers came to a full point of conversion when they came forward for baptism. However, the crucial feature of Wesley's view is that he did not equate regeneration with baptism. "Baptism is not the new

---

[7]   Albert C. Outler, *John Wesley* (New York: Oxford University Press, 1964) 318.

birth: They are not one and the same thing. . . . They do not constantly go together. A man may possibly be 'born of water,' and yet not be 'born of the Spirit.' There may sometimes be the outward sign where there is not the inward grace."[8]

Wesley's "mild allowance" for baptismal regeneration is most evident in his view of infant baptism. He believed infants experience the New Birth in baptism. This does not mean their salvation is guaranteed, as is popularly assumed. Nor is it just a symbolic way of saying they are members of the Christian family and under the care of the church. Rather, it means the baptized child is now actually a Christian in the full sense of the word. Obviously, as baptized children grow up they must be instructed in the faith so they will know what salvation in Christ means. Those who are baptized as infants but later leave the faith must come back to Christ through the normal process of adult conversion. Wesley's view of regeneration as it relates to baptism has been summarized by Rob Staples in the following way.

> To the question, Did Wesley teach baptismal regeneration? The answer is: yes and no. *Yes*, in the case of infants, if it means that the new birth is given in baptism. This assumes, for Wesley, that the church and the believing parents come in faith and obedience to the Lord's command to baptize, promising to give the child the proper Christian nurture and guidance. *Yes*, also, in the case of adults who come to baptism in sincere repentance and faith. . . . *No*, if by the term one means that baptism has some magical or automatic efficacy. Regeneration does not happen just because the rite is performed. . . . *No*, also, if it means that the outward sign (baptism) and the inward grace (the new birth) have been fused together so that the distinction between them is lost and it is held that the two always go together.[9]

Initial Sanctification: Holiness for Beginners

Regeneration is regarded by virtually all Christian traditions as the beginning of the believer's sanctification. Although regeneration and sanctification are not the same thing, they are two aspects of the New Birth: that is, cleansing from the power of sin, and the beginning of spiritual growth. Wesley was in complete harmony with general Protestantism in his view. He did not separate regeneration from sanctification as if they were unrelated, nor did he go to the other extreme of treating them as one and the same. Rather, he

---

[8]   *Works* 6:73–74.

[9]   Rob L. Staples, *Outward Sign and Inward Grace: The Place of Sacraments in Wesleyan Spirituality* (Kansas City: Beacon Hill, 1991) 190–91.

recognized that regeneration is the foundational stage of the sanctification process. In his words, it "is doubtless the gate of it."[10]

Some in the Wesleyan–Holiness tradition have made the mistake of speaking of regeneration and sanctification as if they are independent of each other. The movement is particularly vulnerable at this point due to its emphasis on entire sanctification as a second work of grace which occurs after regeneration. But Wesley saw the whole of sanctification as a comprehensive work of grace that is marked by clearly distinguishable events and stages. Properly understood, these stages may be thought of as distinct works of grace. The first event (or work of grace) in the overall process of sanctification is regeneration. That is why later Wesleyans came to speak of regeneration as initial sanctification. Subsequent stages were then identified as progressive sanctification, entire sanctification, and final sanctification. Although these terms did not come into use until after Wesley's time, they are thoroughly consistent with and grow out of his own doctrine of sanctification. The full spectrum of this doctrine will be treated in the following chapter.

Assurance: Accepting Acceptance

One of the most dynamic contributions made by John Wesley to eighteenth century Christianity was his doctrine of assurance. This was his belief in the direct confirmation of the Holy Spirit to the heart of the believer that the believer is in fact accepted by God and at peace with him. In his sermon "The Witness of the Spirit," Wesley defined Christian assurance as the "inward impression on the soul, whereby the Spirit of God directly witnesses to my spirit, that I am a child of God; that Jesus Christ hath loved me; and given Himself for me; and that all my sins are blotted out; and I, even I, am reconciled to God."[11] Some twenty years after preaching this sermon, Wesley composed a second sermon by the same title. In it he repeats the same definition almost verbatim, followed by the observation that "After twenty years further consideration, I see no cause to retract any part of this."[12] Both sermons were drawn from Romans 8:16: "The Spirit himself testifies with our spirit that we are God's children."

Amazingly, this simple understanding stirred much opposition in Wesley's day. There were two primary reasons. First, it contradicted the standard belief that such intensely personal encounters with the Holy Spirit had ended with the New Testament era. There may be present day exceptions, but they would be very rare and extraordinary cases. Second, even if one did

---

[10]   *Works* 7:205.

[11]   *Works* 5:115.

[12]   Ibid., 124–25.

allow for the possibility of such an experience, the actual practice of it would be liable to all sorts of abuses and excesses. In particular, anyone with such assurance would face the danger of falling into "enthusiasm." This was the common term used in reference to religious fanaticism or extremism. It was a charge Wesley and his followers heard frequently. In an age and culture that revolved around conformity to authority, the charge of enthusiasm was very serious. It fostered exaggerated images of everything from cultish rituals to political subversion. But Wesley argued against both of these objections. He insisted that assurance of salvation is not only freely available to all true Christians, but it should be a normal feature of the believer's experience. It is neither extraordinary nor extremist, but very ordinary and thoroughly biblical.

Wesley's arrival at this understanding of assurance actually developed over many years of deep soul-searching and biblical study. "In fact," says Kenneth Collins, "Wesley's teaching on assurance underwent more modifications and was sustained by more nuances than any other single element in his doctrine of salvation."[13] The fundamental importance of this teaching within Wesley's own spiritual life is illustrated very simply by two of his *Journal* entries that were referred to earlier in Chapter 2. When he first arrived in Georgia in 1736, Wesley sought spiritual counsel from the Moravian pastor August Spangenberg. The pastor shocked Wesley with the question, "Does the Spirit of God bear witness with your Spirit, that you are a child of God?" After a brief and awkward series of evasive answers and further questions, Wesley finally professed meekly that he did have such assurance. He confessed in his *Journal*, however, that "I fear they were vain words."[14] In sharp contrast to this came another entry just two years later following his conversion experience at Aldersgate Street; "an assurance was given me, that he had taken away *my* sins, even *mine*, and saved *me* from the law of sin and death."[15] The depth and subtleties of Wesley's understanding of assurance would mature over the coming decades, but the fundamental core of this doctrine was present at Aldersgate.

But how do believers come to know this assurance? Do they rely on feelings and faith, or is there more to it than that? From Romans 8:16, Wesley identified two different sources or levels of assurance: direct testimony and indirect testimony. First and foremost, there is the direct witness of the Holy Spirit. Simply put, it is an inexpressible inner peace and confidence that one truly is forgiven and accepted by God. It is neither an emotion nor an act of

---

[13]   Collins, *The Scripture Way of Salvation: The Heart of John Wesley's Theology* (Nashville: Abingdon, 1997) 136.

[14]   *Works* 1:36.

[15]   Ibid., 103.

faith. It is an unspoken, inaudible communication from the Holy Spirit in which he bears witness to the person's new life in Christ. Second, in addition to the witness of the Holy Spirit, there is also the witness of the believer's own spirit. This is referred to as the indirect witness. It includes things like practical evidence and rational deductions. It comes from spiritual activities like reading God's promises in the scriptures, uniting with God's people in fellowship and worship, and following God's will in the daily routine of life. If, for example, the fruit of the Spirit—"love, joy, peace, patience, kindness, goodness, faithfulness, gentleness, and self-control" (Galatians 5:22-23)—and other Christian qualities are evident in the believer's life, then he may reasonably conclude that he is redeemed and accepted by God. This is indirect testimony.

Wesley believed there was a particular connection between the fruit of the Spirit and assurance. In fact, he said, there could be no genuine assurance without the fruit of the Spirit. In other words, if a professed believer demonstrates no evidence of Christ-likeness in daily living, then any supposed sense of Christian assurance is an illusion. But, on the other hand, just exhibiting some forms of piety and some evidence of the fruit of the Spirit is not necessarily proof of Christian assurance. For even true pagans can demonstrate aspects of the fruit of the spirit. Therefore, "to ground the assurance only on the fruit is to go back to justification by works."[16] This is why it is essential to understand that the direct witness of the Holy Spirit must always precede the indirect witness of the believer's own spirit. Though the believer's spirit is redeemed, it is still fallen and flawed, and therefore, vulnerable to mistaken impressions. Only the Holy Spirit's direct witness can give true assurance. The indirect witness of the believer's spirit merely helps to confirm that assurance and strengthen his faith.

In his early years, when under the influence of Peter Bohler, Wesley thought people either had faith or they did not. He also thought if they had faith, they would have full assurance. Likewise, if they lacked full assurance, that meant they had no faith. In other words, he failed to see that there are degrees of faith and assurance. When he later came to recognize this, it transformed his life. He then understood that on some days Christians have a greater sense of assurance than they do on other days. In the same way, they have greater and lesser levels of faith at different times. But these fluctuations do not mean they have failed in the faith. Rather, they are simply normal occurrences in the spiritual life of Christians who live in a fallen world.

---

[16] Harald Lindstrom, *Wesley and Sanctification: A Study in the Doctrine of Salvation* (Nappanne, Ind.: Francis Asbury, 1996) 115.

Wesley was passionate in his concern for the spiritual well-being of all believers. Nowhere is that passion revealed more forcefully than his doctrine of Christian assurance. Wesley himself struggled for most of his early life over this issue. He desperately longed for assurance; but since his concept of assurance was faulty, he was always left disappointed and frustrated. His early expectations were unrealistically high and starkly painted in black and white. It was only when he learned to trust the faithful work of the Holy Spirit that he was able to enjoy God's peace within the process of spiritual growth. Regardless of his feelings, he came to accept the remarkable fact that he was accepted by God.

As with all other points of doctrine that came from Wesley, he never saw the doctrine of assurance as anything new. It was simply one of the great biblical and historical truths of the faith that had been neglected and forgotten. He believed one of the reasons why God had raised up the Methodist movement was specifically to revive the preaching and practice of this truth. Wesleyans today maintain that same passion for a Christian faith that rests confidently on the assuring witness of the Holy Spirit.

———•———

Authentic Christianity, in the Wesleyan understanding, is a Christianity of radical transformation. It has nothing to do with straightening out one's life, cleaning up damaging addictions, or taking the moral high ground. These will likely be some of the consequences of that transformation, but they are not the source of it. Christ alone is that source. When people come to him in repentance and faith they enter a new relationship with God and a new life in Christ. They experience absolute forgiveness and acceptance as they are welcomed into God's household as sons and daughters. They are not just treated as sons and daughters, They actually become sons and daughters. Why? Because they have literally been reborn in the image of Christ.

9

The Refinement of Sanctification

Gaining Doctrinal Perspective

Clarifying the Terms

THE THEOLOGICAL language of the doctrine of sanctification can seem obscure. One reason is because various terms related to the doctrine are often used interchangeably. Holiness, perfection, Christian perfection, perfect love, second blessing, second work of grace, heart purity, and filled with the Holy Spirit are just a few common examples. There is nothing necessarily wrong with any of these terms. However, problems do arise when they are used carelessly, for they are not simply different ways of saying the same thing.

To sanctify means to make holy. Therefore, the terms sanctification and holiness carry very close meanings in their broadest sense. All the other terms mentioned above refer to different aspects of the more specific experience of entire sanctification. It was noted in the previous chapter that there are several ways in which the word "sanctification" can be used in reference to Christian experience. When standing alone, it refers to the overall process of being made holy by God. This is a very general usage that includes every aspect of spiritual life from the moment of conversion to the moment of death. But within this wide meaning there are four separate and distinguishable stages of sanctification.

Sanctification begins in conversion. At this stage it is called *initial* sanctification. It is associated with regeneration and the transformation of the New Birth. Acts of sin are forgiven and the new believer enters new life in Christ. It is called initial because it is the beginning point of God's overall work of making the believer holy.

Progressive sanctification is the subsequent process of spiritual growth that the believer experiences through prayer, scripture reading, worship, the

114

sacraments, and fellowship in the church. It is progressive in the sense that it is God's daily work of building holy character in the believer. This is an ongoing process that continues throughout life.

At some point within this lifelong process of progressive sanctification the believer encounters the experience of *entire* sanctification. This event marks a distinct change in the character of the believer's heart. It is the point at which the inner disposition becomes reoriented away from sin and toward God. It is not entire in the sense of achieving a superior status of spirituality, but in the sense of the thoroughness of what God does in the believer's heart. This is a different and more radical work than what God has done previously. The specific nature of this work will be further outlined in the course of this chapter. The significant point here is that entire sanctification is both preceded and followed by the growth of progressive sanctification.

Final sanctification refers to the ultimate state of holiness and separation from sin that will be enjoyed in heaven. A common mistake by many interpreters of Wesley has been the failure to properly recognize his clear distinction between final sanctification and entire sanctification.

Distinctive but Not Unique

The doctrine of entire sanctification is a theological hallmark of Wesleyanism. It receives particular attention because the sanctification of God's people is the ultimate purpose of salvation. God's plan and provision for lost humanity is not just a matter of salvation from eternal punishment; it is about freedom from sin and restoration to the state of fellowship with God that human beings were originally created to enjoy. This means not only forgiving people of their sins, but releasing them from the power and even the very presence of sin—though exactly what that means must be carefully defined.

The general concept of sanctification is a well known biblical teaching that is recognized by all traditions in the Christian faith. No tradition denies that the scriptures call believers to be sanctified. However, the different traditions do have various views on what that call means. Actually, it is more correct to say they have different views on *when* sanctification can be realized by believers. Specifically, they differ over whether holiness is for this life or for the life to come. Wesley was certainly aware of these differences, as evidenced by his observation that "The Papists say, 'This cannot be attained, til we have been refined by the fire of purgatory.' The Calvinists say, 'Nay, it will be attained as soon as the soul and body part.' The old Methodists say, 'It may be attained before we die: A moment after is too late.'"[1]

---

[1] *Works* 8:328.

Wesley's interpretation of the Roman Catholic view is actually incorrect.[2] However, his overall point remains the same. All agreed that since there can be no sin in heaven, a person's heart must be cleansed of all sin before entering heaven. This includes both acts of sin and inherited or original sin. Wesley insisted that the correct biblical teaching is that this cleansing is performed by the Holy Spirit in the present life of the believer, not by the fires of purgatory or the passage of death. This is the primary point at which the Wesleyan concept of entire sanctification becomes a doctrinal distinctive.

Most Protestant interpreters have opted for the position that freedom from sin cannot be realized in this life. Therefore, holiness is interpreted as the ideal, but hopelessly unattainable, goal of spiritual growth. It is presumed to be a future gift that cannot be received until the believer is in heaven. Those who hold to the Calvinistic concepts of sin and imputed righteousness find it especially difficult to allow for actual present holiness. In fact, these two doctrines eliminate even the possibility of such holiness.

Wesley took the biblical mandate for holiness in the literal sense of here and now, even before his Aldersgate Street conversion. He noted that holiness was "the very point at which I aimed all along from the year 1725."[3] It was this emphasis on the call to holiness that caused entire sanctification to be identified as the most distinctive doctrine of Wesleyanism. While Wesleyans gladly accept that entire sanctification is a distinctive doctrine, they strongly refute any notion that it is a unique doctrine. Simply stated, John Wesley did not invent the doctrine of entire sanctification, as any survey of the history of Christian thought reveals.

The doctrine of entire sanctification has been present from the very beginning of the Christian faith. Since the focus of the first few centuries was on the battle against Christological heresies, a systematic doctrine of sanctification did not emerge during that period. Its roots, however, were clearly present in such Early Church Fathers as Irenaeus, Clement of Alexandria, and Origen. By the fourth century the highly regarded writings of Gregory of Nyssa and Macarius the Egyptian (which may also have been written by Gregory), advocated understandings of entire sanctification that sound very Wesleyan.[4] Thomas Oden even goes so far as to assert that the teaching of entire sanctification was so abundant in the ancient church that it can be

---

[2]   J. Kenneth Grider, A *Wesleyan–Holiness Theology* (Kansas City: Beacon Hill, 1994) 456–57.

[3]   *Works* 11:373.

[4]   Paul M. Bassett and William M. Greathouse, *Exploring Christian Holiness*, vol. 2: *The Historical Development* (Kansas City: Beacon Hill, 1985) 69–87.

seen as a unique Wesleyan doctrine only by those with little awareness of the patristic period.[5]

Views compatible with the Wesleyan understanding of entire sanctification were carried forward in later times by men like the medieval Catholic priest Thomas à Kempis, the Protestant Reformers Caspel Schwenkfeld and Thomas Munzer, the Dutch theologian James Arminius, the German Pietist Philipp Jacob Spener, the Quaker founder George Fox, the Anglican bishop Jeremy Taylor, and the English devotional writer William Law. Many of these influences fed into Wesley's heritage and laid the foundation for the development of his thought. In fact, the concept of entire sanctification is so pervasive throughout church history that it can accurately be said that virtually all the major traditions—Orthodox, Catholic, Reformed, and Anglican—played some part in shaping Wesley's passion for holiness.

The Biblical Mandate

Historical precedent may give support to the soundness of a doctrine, but the true source of authority is the Bible. Any study of holiness must begin in the Old Testament. It is there that the basic concepts of God's holiness and humanity's sin are first revealed.

The Old Testament picture of humanity is not pretty. Originally created in God's own image of holiness, humanity quickly fell into sin. In consequence, the human race has been infused with and controlled by sin ever since. When speaking in Genesis 8:21 of humanity's fallen condition, God solemnly declared that "every inclination of his heart is evil from childhood." The psalmist David echoed this assessment when he confessed on behalf of all humanity, "Surely I was sinful at birth, sinful from the time my mother conceived me" (Psalm 51:5). Subsequently, the entire story of the Old Testament is the account of the holy God reaching out to depraved humanity. It is the painstaking story of God's endless efforts to bring his lost creation back to its original state of holiness. The whole point of the Old Testament narrative is not just that God wanted to forgive his people, but that he wanted to forgive them in order to make them holy. He was striving for their sanctification.

By modern standards the Law that was given to Moses at Mt. Sinai appears to be little more than irrelevant trivia from some remote time and place. Even the Ten Commandments are often treated as just a naive goal of moral behavior. But the true purpose of the Law is contained in Leviticus 11:44-45: "I am the LORD your God; consecrate yourselves and be holy, because I am holy. . . . I am the LORD who brought you out of Egypt to be

---

5   Thomas C. Oden, *John Wesley's Scriptural Christianity: A Plain Exposition of His Teachings on Christian Doctrine* (Grand Rapids: Zondervan, 1994) 311.

your God; therefore be holy, because I am holy." This mandate to holiness raises three questions.

First, what does it mean to be holy? In its broadest sense, to be holy is to be sanctified or set apart for God's use. In this regard, virtually anything can be made holy. But the discussion here is specifically on the matter of people being made holy. In the Old Testament there are some seventy references to the holiness of people. In fifty of these cases people are described as being holy in the sense of status or position. For example, priests (Leviticus 21:1-6) and Nazarites (Numbers 6:5, 8) are referred to as holy when fulfilling specific roles. But in the remaining twenty references, holiness is defined in terms of moral righteousness. In other words, there were conditions of conduct and character in the lives of certain people that distinguished them as holy. Although this concept of holiness is used in a minority of the Old Testament references, it is the predominant concept that is used later in the New Testament.[6]

Second, why does God demand that people be holy? The answer, at least in large measure, is fellowship. God desires to draw people into a loving, harmonious relationship. But since God is absolutely holy, he can embrace neither sin itself nor people who are sinful. Therefore, as long as people remain in sin, he cannot enjoy the kind of relationship that he desires. Humanity's alienation actually grieves God. Before God can restore that lost fellowship, he must first make people holy. That is, he must not only forgive sin, he must free people from sin. So the Old Testament command to be holy is far more than a figure of speech, or even an ideal goal. It is an actual condition for fully restored fellowship with God.

Third, how can the keeping of obscure rules and regulations make anyone holy? The answer is not found in the rules and regulations themselves, for no one is made holy by such means. Rather, the answer is found in the concept of obedience. In the Old Testament, obedience is the essence of holiness. It is on the basis of obedience that men like Enoch, Noah, and Abraham, who lived long before the Law of Moses, were accepted by God as holy. So it was not the regulations of the Mosaic Law that made people holy, it was their spirit of faithful obedience that made them holy. This was the standard of measurement. The Law revealed both the nature of God's holiness and the type of character that his holiness requires in people. God required them to live by this code in order for them to gain a basic understanding of the concept of holiness. He needed to teach them that there are clear differences between sin and holiness; between unclean and clean.

---

[6] W. T. Purkiser, *Exploring Christian Holiness*, vol. 1: *The Biblical Foundations* (Kansas City: Beacon Hill, 1983) 31.

The point is this: merely keeping the Law in the technical sense did not make anyone holy. The New Testament Pharisees also kept the Law, but Jesus condemned them for their unrighteousness and hypocrisy. Those who were made holy by God were those who kept the Law in a sincere spirit of love and obedience.

In Deuteronomy 10: 12-13, we find perhaps the most complete definition of holiness in the Old Testament. "And now, O Israel, what does the Lord your God ask of you but to fear the Lord your God, and to walk in all his ways, to love him, to serve the Lord your God with all your heart and with all your soul, and to observe the Lord's commands and decrees that I am giving you today for your own good?" Tragically, the people of Israel failed to grasp the significance of this understanding. Instead, they reduced holiness to a legalistic code of rules and regulations.

The Old Testament gives us the essential building blocks of the biblical call to holiness. It declares that God is holy. It reveals what holiness is. It confirms that humanity was originally holy, but is now sinful. And it affirms that God's greatest desire is to restore humanity to a state of holiness so that intimate fellowship with God can once again be enjoyed. By themselves, however, these building blocks are not enough to develop a full understanding of the call to holiness. To stop here is to risk falling into the same trap of legalism that ensnared so many in the Old Testament. The New Testament must also be read in order to see the full picture of holiness.

The New Testament call to holiness does not contradict the Old Testament; it fulfills it. Jesus quoted the Old Testament when teaching the meaning of holiness. Drawing from Deuteronomy 6:5 and 10:12, he commanded, "Love the Lord your God with all your heart and with all your soul and with all your mind and with all your strength" (Mark 12:30). So while it is true that holiness begins with obedience, it is an obedience rooted in a profound love for God. It is a love that incorporates one's entire being. It is a love that compels people to offer themselves "as living sacrifices, holy and pleasing to God" (Romans 12:1). True holiness is motivated by love rather than obligation.

Peter refers back to the Leviticus passage when he says, "But just as he who called you is holy, so be holy in all you do; for it is written: 'Be holy, because I am holy'" (1 Peter 1:15-16). Although the words are essentially the same, the meaning now takes on an even deeper significance. The life of Jesus and the teachings of scripture reveal that holiness is a condition of the heart. The New Testament concept of holiness begins with the character of Jesus. In him are seen the purity from sin and the absolute love for God that are the hallmarks of holiness. So completely does Jesus encompass holiness that he actually becomes the new definition of holiness. To be holy in the New Testament sense is to be Christ-like.

The call to holiness is pervasive in the New Testament. Even before the beginning of Jesus' public life, John the Baptist highlighted the difference between his own ministry and the ministry of Jesus that would follow. John's ministry was to call people to divine forgiveness: "I baptize you with water for repentance." But Jesus' ministry was to call people to holiness: "He will baptize you with the Holy Spirit and with fire" (Matthew 3:11).

Jesus stated the call very plainly during his Sermon on the Mount: "Be perfect, therefore, as your heavenly Father is perfect" (Matthew 5:48). Later, on the very night he was betrayed, he poured out his passion in a prayer for all those who would come to believe: "They are not of the world, even as I am not of it. Sanctify them by the truth; your word is truth . . . . For them I sanctify myself that they too may be truly sanctified" (John 17:16-19).

The call to holiness was also paramount in Paul's thinking. For example, he urged the troubled church at Corinth: "let us purify ourselves from every-thing that contaminates body and spirit, perfecting holiness out of reverence for God" (2 Corinthians 7:1). He counseled the church at Thessalonica that "It is God's will that you should be sanctified" (1 Thessalonians 4:3). That same letter was then concluded with a blessing for their sanctification: "May God himself, the God of peace, sanctify you through and through. May your whole spirit, soul and body be kept blameless at the coming of our Lord Jesus Christ" (5:23).

A full exposition of the biblical mandate for holiness is beyond the scope and purpose of this survey. However, the scriptural basis of the concept may be summarized in the following points. (1) The Bible identifies two distinct types of sin: *acts of sin*, which need forgiveness; and the *inherent disposition toward sin*, which requires cleansing. (2) The Bible calls all believers to be free from sin; that is, to be holy. (3) In practical terms the Bible defines holi-ness as wholehearted love for God that is best demonstrated through faithful obedience.

The biblical doctrine of holiness may be further considered by focusing on one of its most fundamental aspects—purity of heart.

Blessed Are the Pure in Heart

Moving from Clean to Pure

The process of spiritual cleansing begins at conversion. In that moment of forgiveness and new birth, the repentant sinner is actually cleansed from the guilt and power of sin. But this is only the beginning of God's total work in the believer; for the Bible does not speak only of freedom from sin's guilt and power, it also speaks of freedom from sin itself. This additional cleansing is not a matter of human endeavor any more than the first cleansing. It is, rather, a further demonstration of God's grace at work in the believer. Wesley had this view in mind in his sermon, "The Repentance of Believers":

> Indeed this is so evident a truth, that well high all the children of God, scattered abroad, however they differ in other points, yet generally agree in this—that although we may, "by the Spirit, mortify the deeds of the body;" resist and conquer both outward and inward sin; although we may *weaken* our enemies day by day—yet we cannot *drive them out*. By all the grace that is given at justification we cannot extirpate them. Though we watch and pray ever so much, we cannot wholly cleanse either our hearts or hands. Most sure we cannot, till it shall please our Lord to speak to our hearts again, to speak the second time, "Be clean." And then only the leprosy is cleansed. Then only the evil root, the carnal mind, is destroyed; and inbred sin subsists no more.[7]

The biblical references to a comprehensive cleansing include 2 Corinthians 7:1, Titus 2:14, Ephesians 5:26-27, and 1 John 1:7, to name just a few. The Bible uses many additional words that carry various connotations of cleansing. These include purging, abolishing, rooting out, destroying, and killing. All of these terms are used in one way or another in reference to sin and its consequences. In other words, the Bible is very clear that there is more to salvation than mere release from guilt. God has also made provision for believers to move on to purity of heart.

Wesley believed there is a second call for cleansing because there is a second type of sin—the sinful nature. When a sinner comes to Christ in repentance and faith, all past acts of sin are forgiven. The new Christian is freed from the guilt and power of those sins; but there still remains the inherent tendency toward sin. This corruption of human nature does not need forgiveness, for no one can be held responsible for that which is inherited. Rather, this type of sin requires cleansing.

So when John declares that "If we confess our sins, he is faithful and just and will forgive us our sins and purify us from all unrighteousness" (1 John 1:9), he is speaking to both aspects of sin. He identifies sin that is forgiven and sin that is purified. Thus Wesley is able to confidently answer the question, "Is there no deliverance, no salvation from this inbred sin? Surely there is; else many great and precious promises must fall to the ground."[8] Entire

---

[7]   *Works* 5:165.

[8]   *Works* 12:416.

sanctification, then, is that deliverance from original sin that results in freedom from *both* types of sin.

The Reformed tradition has generally operated from a fundamental belief that freedom from sin in this life is intrinsically impossible. It has, therefore, usually resisted the Wesleyan understanding of heart purity. It has for the most part adhered to the Suppression Theory. This position teaches that the sinful nature remains in the believer, but that God helps the believer to suppress its power and control. Closely related to this is the Keswick Theory. This position also teaches suppressionism, but in a slightly different way. The Holy Spirit fills the believer and counteracts the power of original sin. Although this tradition is not actually Wesleyan, it is closer to Wesleyanism and shares several points of identity with it.

In contrast to these theories, the Wesleyan view is that the Bible teaches an actual cleansing of the inherited sinful nature. In *A Plain Account of Christian Perfection*, Wesley recorded numerous questions and answers on this subject that were discussed at the annual conferences of Methodist preachers. They included the following sets:

> **Q.** Does this imply that all inward sin is taken away?
> **A.** Undoubtedly; or how can we be said to be 'saved from all our uncleanness?' (Ezek. 36:29).[9]
>
> **Q.** When does inward sanctification begin?
> **A.** In the moment a man is justified. (Yet sin remains in him, yea, the seed of all sin, till he is sanctified through-out.)[10]
>
> **Q.** When may a person judge himself to have attained this?
> **A.** When, after having been fully convinced of inbred sin, by a far deeper and clearer conviction than that he experienced before justification, and after having experienced a gradual mortification of it, he experiences a total death to sin, and an entire renewal in the love and image of God.[11]

To be clear, the sin to which Wesley was referring is original sin. And by original sin he meant the corruption of human nature that is demonstrated in two ways: "1. A want of original righteousness; 2. A natural propensity to sin."[12] So Wesley's vision of a pure heart is one that has been restored by the

---

[9]   *Works* 11:387.
[10] Ibid.
[11] Ibid., 401.
[12] *Works* 9:407.

Holy Spirit to God's intended state of righteousness. A chief result of this new righteousness is a new natural propensity to please and obey God.

Baptism with the Holy Spirit

The Wesleyan tradition has an interesting history of internal debate over the relationship of Spirit Baptism to entire sanctification. The fundamental question is whether a believer is baptized with the Holy Spirit at the time of entire sanctification or at conversion.

On the one hand are those who believe that Spirit Baptism is the means through which God carries out the sanctifying work of heart purity. The account of Paul's conversion and subsequent Spirit Baptism is one of the cases that seem to support this view (Acts 9:17). Similarly, the Spirit Baptism of Cornelius (Acts 10:44) has been interpreted as a post-conversion experience.

On the other hand are those who argue that believers receive the Holy Spirit at conversion. In this view, the visit from Ananias is regarded as the point of Paul's conversion. Likewise, Cornelius is understood to have been converted at the time of Peter's preaching.

In fact, the answer is found in both/and rather than either/or. Without doubt, all believers receive the presence of the Holy Spirit at conversion. It is, after all, the Holy Spirit who calls, convicts, and converts the sinner to Christ. However, the *presence* of the Spirit and the *fullness* of the Spirit are not necessarily the same thing. For it is also the Holy Spirit who further calls the believer to the full experience of Christ-likeness. Therefore, it may be accurately said that the believer receives the presence of the Spirit at conversion and the fullness of the Spirit at entire sanctification.

For his part, Wesley did not seem too bothered by either side of the discussion. His attitude was simply; "If they [those who link Spirit Baptism to entire sanctification] like to call this 'receiving the Holy Ghost,' they may: Only the phrase, in that sense, is not scriptural, and not quite proper; for they all 'received the Holy Ghost' when they were justified."[13]

----·----

Entire sanctification is a distinct work of God's grace beyond initial sanctification. In initial sanctification, or conversion, God begins the process of preparing people for heaven. He forgives their acts of sin, makes them righteous, and sets them on a new course with a new life. But this is just the beginning. Wrongful deeds have been forgiven, but the underlying problem

---

[13] *Works* 12:416.

of the heart's inherent bent toward sin remains. This sinful tendency of the heart requires more than forgiveness; it requires cleansing. It requires a work of God's grace that will realign the natural temperament of the heart back toward God. Thus, it is referred to as the experience of heart purity. This is the doctrine Wesleyans call entire sanctification.

The doctrine is rooted in scripture, supported by church tradition, and verified by experience. It is "Wesleyan" only in the sense that it received particular attention and refinement in the thought of John Wesley and the movement that bears his name. It is actually nothing more than the normal Christian experience to which the Bible calls all believers. Therefore, it is accurate to say that what Wesleyans call entire sanctification is, in fact, the common experience of all Christians who sincerely love God with all their heart, soul, mind, and strength. It is the power of grace triumphant over both the power and the presence of sin in the lives of ordinary people. This is authentic Christian experience in the Wesleyan tradition.

10

The Freedom of Perfection

Biblical Images of Perfection

Perfect or Blameless?

SANCTIFICATION IS a two-sided coin. It has both negative and positive aspects, both of which are entirely necessary. The negative dimension refers to what is removed. As the Holy Spirit takes up full residence in the believer's heart, all that is contrary to the Spirit is driven out. The heart is made pure. This, however, is not the end result of sanctification. It is only the negative preparation for the positive which is to follow; that is, the perfection of the heart. For this reason, the concepts of purity and perfection must always be linked together. One does not exist apart from the other.

In spite of the risk of misunderstanding, Wesleyans speak of purity and perfection for one simple reason: both terms come directly from Jesus. Just as he declared, "Blessed are the pure in heart, for they will see God" (Matthew 5:8); so he also commanded, "Be perfect, therefore, as your heavenly Father is perfect" (Matthew 5:48).

Wesley defended his use of the term "perfection" in a 1763 letter: "As to the word 'perfection,' it is scriptural: Therefore neither you nor I can in conscience object to it, unless we would send the Holy Ghost to school, and teach Him."[1] Regardless of this defense, Wesley was actually uncomfortable with the word. He saw how easily it could be misunderstood, but since it is the biblical term he thought it important to continue its use and to teach its proper meaning.

Many contemporary scholars have not shared Wesley's commitment to the biblical terminology. In the Old Testament there are numerous references to the perfection of God and the perfection of humans. But as John Oswalt

---

[1] *Works* 12:257.

points out, the terminology of perfection is usually retained in modern translations only when speaking of God.[2] In references to humans, the words for "perfect" are almost always translated as "blameless." Thus, God is seen as identifying Noah as a blameless man rather than a perfect man (Genesis 6:9). Abraham is called to walk before God and be blameless instead of perfect (Genesis 17:1). And the Israelites as a whole are not commanded to be perfect, but blameless (Deuteronomy 18:13).

The point is not that these translations are necessarily flawed. There is nothing technically wrong with using blameless in place of perfect. Both reflect accurate translations of the original language. Rather, the point is that blameless is a much softer word than perfect. Therefore, it carries a lighter connotation. While it is appropriate to speak of blamelessness as one aspect of the biblical concept of perfection, the current trend in Bible translations leaves a weakened understanding of what the biblical text is actually saying. As Oswalt observes:

> Later versions continue to translate with words for perfection when the reference is to God or his activity, but have abandoned them when the reference is to humans. This does not indicate a new understanding of the meaning of the text, but rather reflects our current despair over human perfectibility. We do not believe such a thing is possible and are therefore reluctant to translate the Bible in such a way as to make it seem so. The fact that the terms are still translated with the words denoting or connoting perfection everywhere but in the case of humans seems to confirm that this is what has happened.[3]

Old Testament Perfection: Character versus Performance

The Old Testament is clear and consistent in its concept of perfection. Whether speaking of God, objects, or people, the meaning is the same. To be perfect is to be whole. That is, it is to be complete and without defect. This definition is readily accepted when thinking of God. He is obviously perfect in all regards. The definition is also accepted when referring to things or objects. In the Mosaic Law, for example, God outlined very specific instructions of what would constitute a perfect animal sacrifice. In order for the sacrifice to be acceptable, the animal had to be perfect. That is, it had to be healthy on the inside and without any blemish or defect on the outside. The sacrificial animal had to be perfect in its character as an animal.

---

[2] John N. Oswalt, *Called to be Holy: A Biblical Perspective* (Nappanee, Ind.: Evangel, 1999) 46.

[3] Ibid.

The same concept of perfection is also applied to people. But if it can be accepted that God required perfection in a goat, why can it not be accepted that God also requires perfection in his people? When God demands a perfect goat, it is understood that he does not require a goat that is perfect in the same way as God. Rather, it is understood that he is referring to a goat that has the perfect character of a goat. There is no thought at all that this is an unrealistic expectation. But when the scriptures speak of perfection in people, the common conclusion is that this is just an ideal, but utterly unrealistic, expectation of humanity. The inconsistency of these two conclusions reflects a deeper inconsistency in our views of perfection.

When the Old Testament speaks of God's perfection it is speaking of his character as God. And when it speaks of an animal's perfection it is speaking of its character as an animal. Therefore, when the Old Testament speaks of a person's perfection it is speaking of that person's character as a human being. Nowhere does the Bible demand the same type of perfection in animals or people that is ascribed to God. Nowhere does the Old Testament suggest that human perfection has anything to do with absolute perfection or life beyond the temptation and potential of sin. Rather, it is very clear that perfection is about being whole in character.

The modern concept of perfection has to do with performance. This understanding is virtually foreign to the Bible. Every reference to God's perfection is a reference to his divine character. It is never a reference to his level of competence in performing his divine duties. The same is true in the biblical references to human perfection. Perfection is about inner quality, not performance. Passages that do speak of perfect activities or a perfect path are actually illustrations of godly character being lived out in daily life. This is apparent, for example, in David's references to his way being perfect (as in 2 Samuel 23:33 and Psalm 101:2, 6).

The Old Testament is filled with God's call to perfection. It is a call that is clear, logical, consistent, and practical. It is neither naive nor unrealistic. It is, in fact, a description of the normal, healthy spiritual life and character of those who belong to God. A perfect person is simply one who possesses and reflects the moral integrity and devotion to God that God desires.

New Testament Perfection: Obedient and Faithful

The New Testament builds on this same understanding of perfection and points to Jesus as the true definition of perfection. But here perfection is not just defined; it is actually revealed and modeled in the person of Jesus. In him we see what it means to be a truly whole person.

It is important to understand that Jesus was not a perfect man because he was divine. Although he was fully divine, he was also fully human. And in order to fulfill the biblical criteria of perfection as a human, he had to actually live in every way as a human. He endured the same kinds of limitations, pains, and temptations that all humans face. But in spite of that, he lived as a perfect person. Therefore, Jesus was not perfect because of his divinity, but because he was obedient and faithful to God as a man.

Jesus never asserted his own will over the will of the Father. His sole purpose was to please the Father by doing what he was sent to do. When challenged by the Pharisees over the validity of his authority, Jesus declared that "The one who sent me is with me; he has not left me alone, for I always do what pleases him" (John 8:29). Likewise, on the night of his betrayal, he affirmed to the Father; "I have brought you glory on earth by completing the work you gave me to do" (John 17:4). Later that same night, just moments before his arrest, he prayed: "Father, if you are willing, take this cup from me; yet not my will, but yours be done" (Luke 22:42). Jesus was perfect in that he obeyed God. The perfect obedience that God had intended for Adam and all his descendents was actually fulfilled in the life of Jesus.

Jesus was also perfect because of his faithfulness. He did not obey the Father only in the technical sense of complying with instructions. He obeyed in the fullest sense of sincere dedication. To be dedicated or consecrated is to offer one's self without reservation. In the case of Jesus this meant, "I lay down my life for the sheep. . . . No one takes it from me, but I lay it down of my own accord" (John 10:15, 18). This fact was certainly not missed by the New Testament writers. Paul noted that "he humbled himself and became obedient to death—even death on a cross!" (Philippians 2:8). The Hebrew letter quotes from Psalm 40 as it portrays Christ as saying, "Here I am, I have come to do your will" (Hebrews 10:9).

The crucial point is that the perfection fulfilled in Jesus is the same kind of perfection to which he calls all believers in Matthew 5:48. This is not the same as saying believers are to possess Christ's perfection. That is impossible. He alone is the divine Son of God, fully human and fully divine. Again, just as a perfect sacrificial goat is not the same as the perfect God, so a perfect Christian is not the same as the perfect Savior.

So, taking into account the Old Testament concept of moral wholeness and the New Testament concept of faithful obedience, what is to be concluded about the overall biblical definition of perfection? Simply this: the essence of Christian perfection is love for God. When believers serve God not just to get to heaven, but because of an inexpressible love for God that compels them to obey his commands and to fulfill his purpose, they have realized the biblical call to perfection.

Wesley's Concept of Perfection

Imperfect Perfection

Wesley was often criticized over his insistence that the Bible teaches a present experience of perfection. He observed that those associated with this doctrine where frequently viewed with distain.[4] Nevertheless, he was convinced that when Christians understood perfection in its proper biblical sense their resistance would melt away. He even found this to be true with his most difficult audience—the Anglican clergy. After explaining his views to the bishop of London in 1740, he was told, "Mr. Wesley, if this be all you mean, publish it to all the world. If anyone then can refute what you say, he may have free leave."[5]

Christian perfection is one of those topics which must first be defined in terms of what it is not before it can be defined in terms of what it is. Wesley learned this lesson and put it into practice. He identified five general ways in which Christians cannot be perfect.[6]

First, perfection does not mean freedom from ignorance. There is no state of grace that ensures faultless knowledge. Entirely sanctified believers have no advantage in this regard. This point may seem trite, but it is actually significant. It refutes any notion of superior biblical or doctrinal knowledge on the basis of an experience of perfection. The pure in heart must study, think, and meditate under the guidance of the Holy Spirit in order to avoid doctrinal errors and misinformation.

Second, perfection does not mean freedom from mistakes. This rules out any association of the doctrine of Christian perfection with performance. Errors in judgment, information, actions, and communication remain throughout life. These are simply some of the many irreversible consequences of living in a fallen world.

Third, perfection does not mean freedom from infirmities. Wesley made frequent references to infirmities. The modern connotation of this word generally implies physical ailment or weakness. While this would certainly be within the realm of Wesley's usage, it falls short of his full meaning. He seems to have in mind "the interaction between the body and the soul and the resultant confusion of thought that can occur."[7] In other words, a perfect heart is not the same as a perfect mind.

---

[4] Albert C. Outler and Richard P. Heitzenrater, eds., *John Wesley's Sermons: An Anthology* (Nashville: Abingdon, 1991) 70.

[5] *Works* 11:374.

[6] *Sermons*, 70–73.

[7] Kenneth J. Collins, *The Scripture Way of Salvation: The Heart of John Wesley's Theology*

Fourth, perfection does not mean freedom from temptation. The struggle with evil is a lifelong battle. There should be no disillusionment over this. However, entire sanctification does make a crucial difference in how the believer responds to temptation. The unsanctified believer still has the disadvantage of a human nature that is naturally inclined to act on temptation. But the entirely sanctified believer has the advantage of a heart that is naturally inclined to resist temptation and turn to Christ for help.

Fifth, perfection does not mean freedom from growth. Perfected Christians still require daily growth in grace. There is no final point of spiritual destination in this life. In this respect, Wesley affirmed that there is no absolute perfection for believers. Spiritual growth remains vital in the experience of perfection. However, it is not quite correct to think of growth as becoming more perfect. Spiritual growth is not movement from one level of perfection to another, but growth within an ever expanding experience of perfection.

Leaving Sin Behind

So what does Christian perfection mean in the Wesleyan understanding? First, it means freedom from willful sin. The emphasis here is on willful. This is not to say that perfected Christians are incapable of sinning. Such Christians can sin and do sometimes sin. Rather, freedom from sin means that through the purifying presence of the Holy Spirit believers are capable of not sinning. In fact, Wesley saw that John's proclamation that "No one who is born of God will continue to sin" (1 John 3:9) was directed to all believers, not just those who adhere to the doctrine of entire sanctification. A life characterized by an absence of willful sin is to be the normal pattern for all who profess the name of Christ.

Second, perfection means freedom from evil thoughts and evil tempers. This expression must not be confused with temptations. Wesley has already asserted that perfection does not exempt people from temptation. This aspect of perfection speaks primarily of attitudes. An evil heart is the source of evil thoughts. Therefore, if the heart is clean, then the thoughts should also be clean. An inner disposition filled with attitudes of resentment, jealousy, anger, contempt, and pride are obviously inconsistent with a heart made pure. As with acts of sin, this is not to say that the sanctified are incapable of harboring such attitudes. It is to say, rather, that such attitudes are now an alien intrusion, not a natural feature.

(Nashville: Abingdon, 1997) 173.

Freedom from deliberate outward sin and freedom from a disposition of inward sin: this is the freedom of Christian perfection. But still Wesley pressed for an even more precise way of defining perfection. When all the biblical components of the concept are considered together—moral wholeness, consecrated obedience, and freedom from the necessity of sin—Wesley arrived at the conclusion which has already been stated. Christian perfection ultimately means unhindered love for God. This is the central theme that echoes through Wesley's various statements of definition on perfection.

> By perfection I mean the humble, gentle, patient love of God, and our neighbor, ruling our tempers, words, and actions.[8]

————•————

> Q. What is implied in being a perfect Christian?
> A. The loving God with all our heart, and mind, and soul.[9]

————•————

> Christians are called to love God with all their heart, and to serve him with all their strength; which is precisely what I apprehend to be meant by the scriptural term perfection.[10]

————•————

> Q. How shall we avoid setting perfection too high or too low?
> A. By keeping to the Bible, and setting it just as high as the Scripture does. It is nothing higher and nothing lower than this—the pure love of God and man; the loving God with all our heart and soul, and our neighbor as ourselves. It is love governing the heart and life, running through all our tempers, words, and actions.[11]

————•————

> Christian perfection is that love of God and our neighbor, which implies deliverance from all sin.[12]

————•————

> Q. What is Christian perfection?

---

[8] *Works* 11:446.
[9] Ibid., 387.
[10] Ibid., 449.
[11] Ibid., 397.
[12] Ibid., 393.

A. The loving God with all our heart, mind, soul, and strength. This implies, that no wrong temper, none contrary to love, remains in the soul; and that all the thoughts, words, and actions, are governed by pure love.[13]

So the Wesleyan concept of Christian perfection is simply the fulfillment of the great command of Moses in the Old Testament (Deuteronomy 6:5; 10:12) and Jesus in the New Testament (Mark 12:30). To love God fully—in heart, soul, mind, and strength—and to live out that love toward others is to fulfill the law of love. This is perfect love. This is Christian perfection.

Event Wrapped in Process

A fundamental question that arises within any discussion of Christian perfection is the issue of how perfection occurs in the heart of the believer. That is, does perfection happen gradually or instantly? Is it a process or a specific event? Wesleyanism is generally understood to be a movement that teaches the instantaneousness of perfection. The expression "crisis experience" has often been used to describe this understanding. Unfortunately, this expression no longer communicates the same idea that it did generations ago. The current connotation of crisis fosters images of a disaster or unexpected emergency that requires urgent attention. But the old connotation of the word simply implied an event that occurred at a specific point in time. Therefore, the old terminology of perfection as a crisis experience was merely a reference to the instantaneous aspect of how perfection is experienced.

The biblical foundation for this understanding is found in the grammatical structures of several key verses. The various terms which express the ideas of entire sanctification, purity, and perfection generally appear in forms that indicate completed action at a specific point.[14] In other words, believers are not called to a process of perfection, but to a completed act of perfection. The nature of the call itself reveals "That this is received merely by faith. . . . That it is given instantly, in one moment."[15]

Students of Wesley may be surprised to discover that he was not fully convinced of instantaneous perfection on the basis of scripture alone. In fact, he thought the scriptures to be somewhat ambiguous on the matter. As he

---

[13]   Ibid., 394.

[14]   For concise explanations of these grammatical forms and their significance to holiness doctrine see J. Kenneth Grider, *Entire Sanctification: The Distinctive Doctrine of Wesleyanism* (Kansas City: Beacon Hill, 1980) 95–97; and Wilber T. Dayton, *A Contemporary Wesleyan Theology: Biblical, Systematic, and Practical*, vol. 1: *Entire Sanctification: The Divine Purification and Perfection of Man* (Grand Rapids: Francis Asbury, 1983) 546–49.

[15]   *Works* 11:393.

put it, "the point is not determined, at least in express terms, in any part of the oracles of God."[16] What did finally convince him was the actual experience of people. Wesley was intensely practical in his approach to theology. And while experience was never the primary source of authority in doctrine, he did believe that experience could help to inform doctrinal understandings. In this spirit of openness, Wesley invested decades of research into real life experiences of faith. This was done primarily through personal interviews. After forty-five years of investigation he reported that he had found no case of anyone professing to have been entirely sanctified in a gradual manner. Instead, those who had a clear testimony of the experience all indicated that it was a specific change of heart that was quite distinct from the normal process of spiritual growth.[17]

In reality, the true Wesleyan understanding is that perfection is both an event and a process. The general pattern of experience indicates a process leading to an event. There is no contradiction in holding to a view of perfection that is both gradual and instantaneous. It is not a matter of choosing one or the other, but of properly embracing both. It is incorrect to say that some people are entirely sanctified through a gradual process while others are sanctified in a moment. Everyone is sanctified through both a process and in a moment. The difference is that some have a more intense experience of process and a more subtle experience of crisis; while others experience only a brief or faint sense of process and a more obvious and dramatic moment of crisis.

Wesley uses the analogy of death to make this point. "A man may be dying for some time; yet he does not, properly speaking, die, till the soul is separated from the body; and in that instant he lives the life of eternity. In like manner, he may be dying to sin for some time; yet he is not dead to sin till sin is separated from his soul."[18] Some people die suddenly and dramatically. Others die after a long process of disease or old age. In those cases death may even be so gradual as to seem imperceptible to those looking on. However, there is still a specific moment when death occurs and the person's state of being is radically changed. Wesley saw this analogy of death as a helpful way to visualize how entire sanctification (and its corresponding work of perfection) is both a process and an event.

In 1764, Wesley reflected on his years of study and teaching on the subject of Christian perfection. He summarized the doctrine in the following eleven points.

---

16   *Works* 6:490.
17   Ibid., 491.
18   *Works* 11:402.

(1) There is such a thing as perfection; for it is again and again mentioned in the Scripture.

(2) It is not so early as justification; for justified persons are to 'go on unto perfection' (Heb. 6:1).

(3) It is not so late as death; for St. Paul speaks of living men that were perfect (Phil. 3:15).

(4) It is not absolute. Absolute perfection belongs not to man, nor to angels, but to God alone.

(5) It does not make a man infallible. None is infallible while he remains in the body.

(6) Is it sinless? It is not worth while to contend for a term. It is 'salvation from sin.'

(7) It is 'perfect love' (1 John 4:18). This is the essence of it: its properties, or inseparable fruits are rejoicing evermore, praying without ceasing, and everything giving thanks (1 Thess. 5:16, etc.).

(8) It is improvable . . . one perfected in love may grow in grace far swifter than he did before.

(9) It is amissable, capable of being lost; of which we have numerous instances.

(10) It is constantly both preceded and followed by a gradual work.

(11) But is it in itself instantaneous or not? . . . . An instantaneous change has been wrought in some believers: None can deny this. . . . But [others] did not perceive the instant when it was wrought. It is often difficult to perceive the instant when a man dies; yet there is an instant in which life ceases. And if ever sin ceases, there must be a last moment of its existence, and a first moment of our deliverance from it.[19]

———•———

Wesley was fully aware of the controversial nature of his teaching on Christian perfection. What was controversial, however, was not so much that he spoke about it, but that he actually accepted it at face value. Rather than inventing a more comfortable interpretation, he simply followed his usual principle of taking the Bible in its most obvious sense. Wesley felt he had no choice but to deal straight on with the admittedly difficult command of Jesus to "Be perfect, therefore, as your heavenly Father is perfect" (Matthew 5:48). He

---

[19]   Ibid., 441–42.

was constantly searching for better, simpler, clearer ways of expressing this aspect of biblical theology. His most concise definition was stated in just two words—perfect love.

Part 3

The Wesleyan Vision
Practical Holiness in the Real World

11

The Experience of Holiness

Entering the Holy Life

Receiving Entire Sanctification

DIFFERENT PEOPLE tell different stories of how they entered the experience of entire sanctification. For some there is more awareness of a long process than a precise event. For others, a specific point in time stands out clearly as their moment of entire sanctification. Likewise, some enter the experience with a greater sense of need for purity of heart, while others are more conscious of the need for perfection of love. Consequently, these different people may see the necessary steps to holiness in different ways. This does not mean, however, that the experience is a purely subjective matter for each individual. In fact, scripture and experience together do reveal certain essential elements that are typically involved in the steps toward holiness.

First, there arises in the believer a consciousness of further need in the spiritual life that goes beyond forgiveness of sin. Some believers may experience this awareness as conviction over the failure to cope appropriately with temptation. Others may experience an unquenchable thirst for the deeper things of God. Still others may be wrestling with spiritual restlessness or lack of peace. It must be understood that this sense of deeper need is not the same as the sense of guilt that accompanied conviction prior to conversion. The person pursuing holiness already knows release from the guilt of sin. Rather, this sense of need may be described as conviction of the inner inclination toward sin. As Wesley put it, "It is properly a conviction, wrought by the Holy Ghost, of the sin which still remains in our heart; . . . even in them that are regenerate. . . . It is a conviction of the tendency of our heart to self-will."[1]

---

[1] *Works* 6:50.

Second, the believer responds to this awareness of need through prayer. This is not a prayer of repentance in the same sense as was prayed at conversion; nonetheless, it is genuine repentance. Kenneth Collins explains: "On the one hand, this evangelical repentance is in some respects similar to the earlier legal repentance in that it entails both contrition and considerable self-knowledge. On the other hand, it is different in that one repents not of actual sin—from which the regenerated believer has already been set free—but of inbred sin."[2] This type of repentance may best be described as a prayer of sorrow over not being more fully conformed to the image of Christ. It is a prayer in which the believer expresses the heart's deepest desire to obey and please God in every possible way.

Third, this prayer of remorse then becomes a prayer of consecration. In this the believer renews and deepens his devotion to God. Depending again on the particular experience of the believer up to this point, this time of consecration may be thought as an act of surrender, or a vow of dedication, or a pledge of ultimate loyalty. In reality, consecration involves all of these and more. The end result is a death of self-centeredness and an awakening to God-centeredness. It is moving beyond the self-oriented focus of having sins forgiven, and moving into the God-oriented focus of truly giving over to him every part of one's being. This surrendering of self to the total and absolute will of God is what Wesleyans refer to theologically as the purifying and perfecting of the heart.

Fourth, there is an exercise of faith. Just as justification is accepted by faith at the time of conversion, so also heart purity and perfection are accepted at the time of entire sanctification. This moment may be a very dramatic landmark on the believer's spiritual journey or it may be more subtle. Either way, it is just as significant. God has performed a further miracle of grace in the heart of the believer.

It must be stressed that the scenario just described is not a four step plan to sanctification. It is merely a general account of the progression typically encountered by those who enter the experience of holiness. However, those moving through this process of faith may not even be consciously aware of the phases. They may simply see the entire encounter as an indescribable hunger and thirst for God that brings them into an experience whereby they can truly say they love God with all their heart, soul, mind, and strength. And because of this intense love for God, they discover that they also love their neighbor.

Wesley tried to illustrate the process of Christian experience by comparing it to a house. We are brought to the porch by prevenient grace. We

---

[2]   Kenneth J. Collins, *John Wesley: A Theological Journey* (Nashville: Abingdon, 2003) 191.

140

enter the door through conversion. We are welcomed into all the magnificent rooms of the entire structure through sanctification. The manner in which different individuals will make the transition from first entry through the front door to the vast resources God's house cannot be precisely calculated or prescribed. The Holy Spirit invites, welcomes, and guides different people in different ways, though the overall process follows this general pattern.

The Evidence of Entire Sanctification

The issue of evidence naturally arises in any discussion of how one enters the holy life. The question is straightforward. How do people know they have been entirely sanctified? The answer is not straightforward. The peril is in the tendency of people to search for external evidences. This can result in anything from legalism to emotionalism to spiritual pride.

Wesley correctly understood that the evidences of sanctification are internal, though they will ultimately find external expressions. Even at that, his answer to the question of evidence seems daunting at first glance:

> **Q.** By what 'fruit of the Spirit' may we 'know that we are of God,' even in the highest sense?
>
> **A.** By love, joy, peace, always abiding; by invariable long suffering, patience, resignation; by gentleness, triumphing over all provocation; by goodness, mildness, sweetness, tenderness of spirit; by fidelity, simplicity, godly sincerity; by meekness, calmness, evenness of spirit; by temperance, not only in food and sleep, but in all things natural and spiritual.[3]

Wesley's intent was not to create a spiritual checklist, but to point out that the only true evidence of entire sanctification is the disposition of the heart. A person who is outwardly pious may have the appearance of holiness while inwardly harboring very unholy attitudes. Likewise, a new convert may seem far from perfection in the outward sense, while actually displaying an inner spirit of true humility and holiness before God. Wesley even acknowledged that there may be cases where a newly justified believer genuinely possesses these qualities of holiness from the very moment of conversion. He immediately cautioned, however, that such cases are exceptional. The usual sequence is that entire sanctification follows sometime after the point of conversion.

More will be said about the relationship between the fruit of the Spirit and entire sanctification in the next chapter. Wesley saw that relationship as

---

[3] *Works* 11:422.

absolutely vital; for not only is it the truest inward evidence of holiness, it is also the truest outward expression of holiness.

Some segments of the Pentecostal tradition teach that "speaking in tongues" is the only real evidence of sanctification and Spirit Baptism. Although much of the Pentecostal movement shares a common heritage with the Wesleyan movement, the two traditions disagree on this point. Wesley rejected the modern notion of speaking in tongues. He held instead to the traditional understanding that the biblical references to this phenomenon are accounts of the God-given ability to suddenly speak a foreign language for the purpose of preaching and evangelism. But whatever definition of "speaking in tongues" is used, the Wesleyan tradition has never identified this one spiritual gift as the evidence of entire sanctification or Spirit Baptism. For Wesley, the truest evidence of inner holiness is always summed up in whole-hearted love for God.

Sin and the Holy Life

Expectations and Reality

Even though the language of cleansing and purity is clearly biblical, it can also be troublesome. On the one hand, it has led some to mistakenly expect unrealistic results. On the other hand, it has deterred others from expecting any results at all. Although Wesley tried to maintain a proper balance between these two overreactions, it must be acknowledged that he too leaned toward unrealistic expectations at times. For example, when describing the qualities of a purified heart he once wrote:

> They are freed from self-will, as desiring nothing but the holy and perfect will of God: not supplies in want, not in ease of pain, nor life, or death. Or any creature; but continually crying in their inmost soul, 'Father, they will be done.' They are freed from evil thoughts, so they cannot enter into them . . . They are free from wanderings in prayer. Whensoever they pour out their hearts in a more immediate manner before God, they have no thought of anything past, or absent, or to come, but of God alone.[4]

While the description of a heart that is free from self-will and desires God's will is clearly biblical, the claim that evil thoughts cannot enter is not. Wesley later recognized this and added two footnotes to these comments. In the first note he criticized his statement that the pure in heart do not seek to ease their pain. He said, "This is too strong. Our Lord Himself desired

---

4   *Works* 6:379.

ease in pain. He asked for it only with resignation: 'Not as I will,' I desire, 'But as Thou wilt.'" In the second footnote he completely denounced his assertion that the pure in heart are free from wandering thoughts during prayer. He remarked, "This is far too strong. See the sermon 'On Wandering Thoughts.'"[5] To his credit, Wesley was willing to censure and correct his own earlier opinions. On the whole, he maintained expectations that where biblically sound and sensibly practical, in spite of isolated comments that appear to indicate otherwise.

Wesley's later followers did not always heed his example in striving for balance between expectations and reality. At one extreme were those who set expectations so low that the entire concept of sanctification was rendered meaningless. They consequently minimized the doctrine and abandoned the teaching of heart purity as a biblical mandate. Entire sanctification became confused with progressive sanctification and was equated with spiritual growth. Cleansing from the inward nature of sin was explained in terms of suppression rather than freedom.

At the other extreme were those who exaggerated the results of Christian perfection beyond all reasonableness. Expectations were set so high that sanctification was rendered unobtainable. Those who fell into this trap often portrayed heart purity and perfection as a nearly angelic state of absolute sinlessness. Sin was frequently viewed as something that could simply be isolated and destroyed, never to return again. While it is true that the Bible uses terms and images along these lines, it must be remembered that they are just that—terms and images. They are illustrations of what sin is like. In fact, sin is not a thing at all. It is primarily a broken relationship that results in alienation from God. So when the Bible speaks of the heart being cleansed or purified from sin, it is speaking of the profound change of heart in which the Christian's remaining spirit of self-centeredness is transformed into a new spirit of God-centeredness.

In surprising contrast to the popular image of Wesley as the stern disciplinarian with lofty ideals of Christian perfection, it was actually Charles who had to be cautioned about the dangers of unrealistic expectations. John wrote to him in 1766; "That perfection which I believe, I can boldly preach; because I think I see five hundred witnesses of it. Of that perfection which you preach, you think you do not see any witness at all. . . . [T]o set perfection so high is effectively to renounce it."[6]

So what actually is the essence of heart purity? According to the scriptures it is love for God and obedience to his will. To repeat again the words

---

[5]   Ibid.
[6]   *Works* 12:131.

of Jesus, to be pure in heart is to "Love the Lord your God with all your heart and with all your soul and with all your mind and with all your strength" (Mark 12:30).

The Meaning of Sinlessness

The Wesleyan belief in freedom from the inherent inclination toward sin is sometimes mistakenly cited as proof that Wesleyans teach sinless perfection. The image portrayed is that of a spiritual plateau that lifts the entirely sanctified beyond the reach of sin. Of course no Christian tradition, Wesleyan or otherwise, teaches that such a plateau exists in this life. Wesley emphatically rejected this notion. It is true that he did teach a type of sinlessness, but this is a relative concept that must be understood in the context of its intended meaning.

There are basically two different senses in which it is correct to say that Wesleyans believe in sinlessness. First, there is the abandonment of sin to which all believers are called: "No one who lives in him keeps on sinning. No one who continues to sin has either seen him or known him" (1 John 3:6). The biblical teaching of justification, forgiveness, and new life in Christ clearly indicates that a sinless life is to be the normal pattern for all believers. So, in this sense, Wesleyans do teach a type of sinlessness, but only the type overtly proclaimed in the Bible.

Second, Wesleyans believe in sinlessness in the sense of having the inherited tendency toward sin cleansed from the heart. This too is a type of sinlessness that is taught in scripture. Believers are called to a further work of God's grace that transforms the natural impulse toward sin into a natural impulse toward God.

There is, however, a third type of sin from which there is no escape in this life—the sin Wesley called involuntary sin. These are sins of ignorance, mistake, and human limitation. They are involuntary in that they are unintentional. Wesley's important insight was that while all sin is an offense against God, all offenses are not necessarily sin. If a man knowingly passes along false information, he is sinful. However, if he passes along the same information without knowing it is false, then he is not sinful; he is only mistaken.

The life of holiness is sinless in regard to deliberate acts of sin, but it is not sinless in the sense of absolute perfection. This is why Wesleyans can speak of a relative form of sinlessness without embracing a false notion of sinless perfection. It is also why they can, without contradiction, both testify to freedom from sin and offer prayers of confession for involuntary sins.

The danger in Wesley's understanding of sin is that it can be abused by those who desire to treat sin lightly. Those who wish to avoid the ugly reality of true sin in their life may think they can simply dismiss that sin by calling it involuntary or a mere infirmity of the flesh (to use Wesley's expressions). Of course, calling sin by some other name does not negate the fact that it is still sin.

Backstepping Sin

In light of the biblical call to sinlessness, what is to be made of the fact that entirely sanctified Christians do sometimes commit acts of willful sin? Does this mean they were never sanctified? Does it prove that sanctification does not actually work in the real world? Does it confirm the hopeless nature of the believer's battle against sin? For Wesley these questions were never an issue. He always accepted that sanctification did not mean freedom from the possibility of sin. It only meant freedom from the necessity of sin. This is the crucial distinction that is often missed.

Still, the fact remains that the entirely sanctified do sometimes sin. Why? Because of the nature of freedom. On the one hand, the sanctified *do not* have freedom from temptation; but on the other hand, they *do* have freedom either to resist temptation or to act on it. Sin always remains an option, though not a necessity. Theodore Runyon helpfully points out that "Wesley saw no inconsistency in the claim that the root of sin is removed, and yet the entirely sanctified are not beyond temptation. The fact that temptation no longer comes from the substance of sin within does not exclude temptations from without, just as was the case with the progenitors of the race, Adam and Eve."[7] Leo Cox captured the essence of it even more succinctly: "Christ was holy and He was tempted. Adam was holy; he was tempted and fell. The entirely sanctified are holy, but they are tempted and may fall."[8]

Occasional lapses into sin are inevitable in the justified Christian because the sinful nature that remains in the heart is continually drawing the convert back toward the old patterns of sin. But in the entirely sanctified Christian, such lapses are possible, but no longer inevitable since the new nature of the heart is drawn toward pleasing God.

In spite of his insistence that sin is not inevitable in the sanctified life, Wesley was keenly aware of the struggle. He sometimes quoted statistics on the percentage of sanctified believers who had fallen from that state of holiness through willful acts of sin. These do not appear to have been figures

---

[7] Theodore Runyon, *The New Creation: John Wesley's Theology Today* (Nashville: Abingdon, 1998) 100.

[8] Leo G. Cox, *John Wesley's Concept of Perfection* (Kansas City: Beacon Hill, 1964) 167.

based on actual records, but only on Wesley's impression at the time. In his most pessimistic moments he claimed that just one in thirty managed to maintain an experience of freedom from sin. In his more optimistic moods he raised the number to one in three. The point is that the Wesleyan understanding of perfection always acknowledges the possibility of recurrent sin. But a brief lapse into sin does not mean the end of one's faith or experience. For the grace that brings people to Christ in the first place and draws them to the life of holiness is the same grace that restores those who fall. In 1770, Wesley wrote to a woman who was struggling to keep her faith alive and to renew the lost peace of a formerly sanctified heart:

> Just now we have many persons all over England that are exactly in the state you describe. They were some time since renewed in love, and did then rejoice evermore; but after a few years, months, or weeks, they were moved from their steadfastness: Yet several of these have within a few months recovered all they had lost, and some with increase; being far more established than ever they were before. And why may it not be so with you? . . . Surely you should be every day expecting the same free gift; and He will not deceive your hope.[9]

Wesley used the term "backsliding" to describe the experience of those who fall back into sin. By this he meant the slips that commonly accompany the spiritual journey, even in the sanctified life. A sanctified believer momentarily loses spiritual footing when he sins. He "slides" backward until the Holy Spirit catches him through conviction of heart and enables him to regain his footing. Unfortunately, many later Wesleyans missed this meaning in their concept of backsliding. They focused solely on the believer's sin while ignoring the Holy Spirit's response. Backsliding came to be seen in a far more literal sense than Wesley intended; a sense in which a single act of sin sent the believer plummeting all the way back to a preconverted state. Thus, the entire spiritual journey had to start over again from a new point of conversion. These later Wesleyans failed to understand that backsliding, like sanctification, is both a process and an event, only in reverse order. As Wesley summarized it; "love grows cold before it is lost; faith weakens before it ceases."[10]

Perhaps a more helpful imagery than backsliding is that of backstepping. This is actually what Wesley had in mind. When a sanctified believer sins, the spiritual journey is disrupted and comes to a halt. The Holy Spirit immediately brings conviction to the heart and gives immediate opportunity for repentance. If the person responds obediently with sincere repentance,

---

[9] *Works* 12:389.
[10] Cox, *Perfection*, 169.

then fellowship is restored and the journey continues. In other words, there has been no backsliding. If, however, the person resists the Holy Spirit's correction, then he has reverted back to an attitude of rebellion against God. Now he has taken a deliberate step backward from God. Once again the Holy Spirit convicts. If the person once again resists, then he has taken yet another step backward from God. If this process continues then the person is truly backsliding. But the important thing to recognize is that the first act of sin is not, technically speaking, backsliding. It only sets the stage for backsliding. The actual backsliding is the subsequent pattern of disobedience to the Holy Spirit's call for repentance.

So, even though willful sin may enter a sanctified believer's heart, all is not lost. The One who was faithful and just to forgive sin at conversion is equally faithful and just to forgive sin at any stage along the path of the spiritual journey. An isolated lapse into sin does not mean a return to the point of origin in the journey. The Holy Spirit convicts at the point of offense, and God forgives at the point of offense; provided there has been a response of obedience and repentance. Thus, the journey continues on from the point of disturbance.

Avoiding Sin

Of course, the way to avoid the dilemma of sin in the sanctified life is to avoid sin itself. Wesley saw that the first step toward making oneself vulnerable to the temptations of sin was the neglect of daily devotions. Wesley was famous for rising at 4:00 AM in order to spend the first hour of the day in prayer and mediation. (He frequently preached his first sermon of the day at 5:00 AM) But what some may regard as an excessive display of self-discipline, Wesley regarded as essential food for the soul. He understood that a believer who loves God with all his heart, soul, mind, and strength, will naturally want to spend time alone with God. He also understood that such a believer is very unlikely to suddenly and abruptly succumb to temptation. Rather, those who fall into sin usually do so by slowly drifting closer and closer to the brink of danger. This drifting is usually the result of sins of omission. That is, the neglect of things like prayer, scripture reading, corporate worship, and acts of goodness.

Perhaps the most significant aspect of Wesleyan theology that is routinely missed is the moment-by-moment character of the holy life. Wesley believed and taught an instantaneous experience of entire sanctification. However, his intended meaning in this doctrine is utterly lost if his emphasis on the momentary aspect of holiness is overlooked. Entire sanctification does not make believers instantly holy for the rest of life any more than it makes them absolutely sinless. Rather, it makes them holy and sinless in the present moment and then enables them to renew and nourish that holiness into the next moment and the next and the next.

———•———

Authentic Christianity in the Wesleyan tradition is a Christianity that pursues holiness. It is a Christianity that seeks holiness and nurtures holiness in the midst of a busy and chaotic life. The experience of holiness is not about forgiveness of sin, but about freedom from sin. It is the radical reorientation of the human heart away from self-centeredness and toward God-centeredness—away from sin and toward righteousness.

12

The Expression of Holiness

Spiritual Fruit and Gifts

Character over Words

THE PRACTICAL question of how holiness is actually expressed in daily life is a critical component of any study of the doctrine. Wesley was well aware of the importance of this question. The essence of his response was that true holiness will be expressed through the very character of who we are and how we live. Beyond that he was hesitant to give specific answers to the question. He was very cautious, for example, on the matter of personal testimony. He warned the early Methodists that they should not discuss their experience of entire sanctification with the unconverted, or even with those who were converted but were not seeking the experience. The reason for this caution was very practical. Wesley knew that claims of personal holiness would be misunderstood by those who did not already believe in it. Therefore, matters of personal testimony and experience were to be discussed only with those who either knew the experience for themselves or were sincerely seeking to know it.

Perhaps this helps to explain why Wesley himself never recorded any direct or explicit personal testimony of his own experience of entire sanctification. Some have inferred from his silence that he did not actually have the experience himself. It seems more likely that his silence was simply a matter of following his own advice. He realized that every detail of his life was under intense public scrutiny. Therefore, any personal claim to holiness would only open the floodgates for further attack on his character and ministry.

So what was Wesley's understanding of how to appropriately express holiness of heart and life? It was simply to live an authentic Spirit-filled life in the ordinary routine of each day. The undeniable witness of true holiness is the change of attitudes, words, and actions that naturally flows from the transformed heart. This is the function of the Holy Spirit's cleansing and empowering presence in the sanctified believer. In his famous sermon, *Scriptural Christianity*, Wesley said the filling of the New Testament apostles with the Holy Spirit was for this very purpose.

> It was, to give them . . . the mind which was in Christ, those holy fruits of the Spirit . . . to fill them with "love, joy, peace, longsuffering, gentleness, goodness" (Gal. 5:22-24); to endue them with faith . . . with meekness and temperance: to enable them to crucify the flesh . . . and, in consequence of that inward change, to fulfil all outward righteousness; to "walk as Christ also walked," in "the work of faith, in the patience of hope, the labour of love" (1 Thess. 1:3).[1]

A contemporary tendency is to think that the primary purpose of the Holy Spirit's presence is to bestow spiritual gifts. But Wesley correctly understood that the Spirit's primary purpose is to bestow the mind of Christ. It is the mind of Christ that then produces the fruit of the Spirit. And it is the fruit of the Spirit that demonstrates the presence of the Spirit in the ordinary routine of life.

The clear definition of this spiritual fruit is provided in Galatians 5:22-23: "the fruit of the Spirit is love, joy, peace, patience, kindness, goodness, faithfulness, gentleness and self-control. Against such things there is no law." It is important to notice that the Bible does not speak of the fruits (plural) of the Spirit, but of the fruit (singular) of the Spirit. That is to say, the fruit is a unified whole. The Spirit does not give some parts of the fruit to some believers and other parts to other believers. That is true of the spiritual gifts, but it is not true of the fruit. The nine elements of the fruit of the Spirit comprise a single fruit that is evident to at least some degree in all believers. For those who are entirely sanctified, the healthy development of the fruit becomes the true expression of holiness. Although the fruit is a single unit, the nine elements may be categorized according to three general aspects of the Christian life—walking with God, relating to others, and developing character.

Walking with God

Love is the first component of the fruit of the Spirit. This commonly used word must be understood in terms of its proper meaning; for this is not love in the popular sense of emotion or infatuation, but love in the sense that Jesus taught. It is the loving of God with all the heart, soul, mind, and strength. This is the core of the spiritual fruit. At the center of everything Wesleyans believe about holiness is this concept of pure love for God. Without this love

---

[1]   *Works* 5:38.

for God there can be no fruit of the Spirit; and without the fullness of the Holy Spirit there can be no pure love for God.

Love is followed by *joy*. When the believer is enabled by the Holy Spirit to truly love God, the experience of that intimacy with the Creator naturally produces joy. Of course, this is not merely the emotion of feeling happy or upbeat. It is the deeply rooted awareness and acceptance of God's love for us and our response of love that goes back to him. For this reason the source of true joy can only be found in God.

In his classic spiritual autobiography, *Surprised by Joy*, C. S. Lewis confessed that the essence of his life was his search for joy; "for in a sense the central story of my life is about nothing else."[2] But Lewis did not think of joy in theological terms. He could only describe it as:

> an unsatisfied desire which is itself more desirable than any other satisfaction. I call it Joy, which is here a technical word and must be sharply distinguished both from Happiness and from Pleasure. Joy (in my sense) has indeed one characteristic, and only one, in common with them; the fact that anyone who has experienced it will want it again.[3]

Lewis eventually found the joy he sought, but not where he expected it. He thought joy would be found in "a place"—that is, a particular event, experience, or circumstance. "Instead," he said, "I found it to be a Person."[4] He found joy when he surrendered to God.

Just as love produces joy, so joy gives rise to *peace*. The essence of peace is assurance or security. It is the fundamental confidence of being embraced in God's love, forgiveness, and protective care. Wesley saw that peace is about reconciliation with God. "It is a peace that banishes all doubt, all painful uncertainty; the Spirit of God bearing witness with the spirit of the Christian, that he is 'a child of God.'"[5] This banishment of doubt and uncertainty does not mean that all questions are fully answered. It only refers to the specific question of acceptance by God through Christ. It is the assurance of that acceptance. No one can do anything to instill peace within their own heart. It is a gift from God. Individuals do, however, have the power to destroy inner peace. They can destroy it by willfully breaking fellowship with God, by failing to trust him in times of difficulty, or by simply refusing to believe that they are in fact reconciled to him.

---

2 C. S. Lewis, "Surprised by Joy," in *The Inspirational Writings of C. S. Lewis* (New York: Inspirational, 1994) 11.

3 Ibid.

4 Ibid., 126.

5 *Works* 5:80.

Relating to Others

Patience is unique among the virtues of the Spirit's fruit in that it is a passive virtue. All the other virtues are active. They address things people do, either by word, thought, or deed. Patience speaks to what people do not do. It is not just a matter of waiting quietly in the face of frustration. It actually carries the much deeper meaning of not seeking revenge or taking retaliatory action when it is within one's power, and even right, to do so. The best way to understand the meaning of patience is simply to examine how God responds to humanity. He responds to sin with patience. He responds to failure with patience. He responds to misunderstanding with patience. Even when people turn on him and accuse him of being the cause of their problems, he still responds with patience. It is clearly within both his power and his right to respond otherwise. Instead, he patiently calls people back to himself and patiently waits for their acknowledgment of his presence. God's patience is not about what he does, it is about what he does not do. This is the same passive spirit that is to guide Christians in their interaction with those they encounter.

Where patience resides *kindness* naturally follows. Kindness may be either active or passive. Sometimes the truly kind response is no response at all, as with patience. Other times kindness can be displayed only by definite action, as in a kind word or deed offered for the benefit of others. The primary characteristic of kindness is its selflessness. It is doing what is best for others without thought of personal gain or benefit. The Good Samaritan is the epitome of kindness; going out of his way, beyond his usual boundaries, and at cost to himself to be of service to another. If he had not bothered to inconvenience himself no one would have known or cared. Even if someone had known, they would not have criticized him, for he would have been doing what was normally expected in such a circumstance. His response was a true demonstration of kindness.

Goodness may be thought of as kindness on a larger and deeper scale. Kindness can be reflected in good deeds, but goodness itself is a more fundamental aspect of a person's character. It is a quality of the heart that permeates every aspect of one's interaction with others. The interesting thing about this word is that it is unique to the New Testament in the ancient Greek language. That is, it does not appear in any secular Greek literature of that era. While specific acts of kindness were well known, the more fundamental concept of goodness as a quality of life and a characteristic of human relationships was not known. Of course, this is not to say that there were no truly good people before that time. The point is that the pagan Greek culture of the New Testament age had no word equivalent to the biblical word for goodness.

Developing Character

The elements of the fruit of the Spirit that influence the development of personal character begin with *faithfulness*. Obviously, the concept of faithfulness comes from that of faith. But whereas faith has a theological connotation, faithfulness has an ethical or behavioral connotation. Faith has to do with belief and the exercise of trust. Faithfulness has to do with being believable and trustworthy. It is about being reliable, authentic, and sincere. The faithfulness of God is demonstrated continually throughout the entire Bible. The Old Testament develops this theme as the history of Israel is recounted. The New Testament expands the story to include God's faithful pursuit of all lost humanity through the redemptive work of Christ. The message of the Bible is that God is to be believed because he is believable; he is to be trusted because he is trustworthy. These are qualities that Christians are to demonstrate in their relationship with God and with others.

Gentleness is the more modern term for what may also be translated as meekness. Gentleness is the preferred word because of the undertone of weakness that is usually associated with meekness. In fact, meekness, or gentleness, is the ultimate display of strength. It is the voluntary submission to a higher principle—the principle of Christ-likeness. It is the result of love, joy, peace, patience, kindness, and goodness. It is not forced or unnatural. In fact, it cannot be forced or unnatural, otherwise it is not gentle. Gentleness is a gift from God and a work of his grace. But just as gentleness must not be confused with weakness, so also it must not be equated with timidity. For the words and actions of men like Peter and Paul or Wesley and Whitefield make it clear that they were men of strength and boldness, both physically and spiritually, who were not easily intimidated. Yet they were incredibly gentle. They bear out the truth of the saying that nothing is as strong as true gentleness, and nothing is as gentle as true strength.

The fruit of the Spirit culminates in *self-control*. Whereas gentleness is the voluntary surrender to the principle of Christ-likeness, self-control is the voluntary mastery of desires for the sake of Christ. It is the disciplined determination to resist the temptation of re-enthroning self as the centerpiece of existence. Self-control is the ability to master both appetites and ambitions. But in spite of the way it sounds, self-control is also a gift of God's grace, not a virtue of human effort. Left to themselves people are utterly incapable of genuine self-control. That is why the fruit of the Spirit ends with self-control rather than beginning with it. Self-control is made possible only as the other eight components of the fruit are received and lived out. The other virtues feed and nourish self-control. In return, self-control is used by the Holy Spirit to preserve, activate, and develop the other eight. Thus the fruit is able to grow and fulfill its purpose—the purpose of glorifying God through the Spirit-filled lives of ordinary people.

The fruit of the Spirit defines the Spirit-filled believer's essential nature. Characteristics that reflect this fruit become expressions of true holiness. There will be no need to manufacture displays of holy piety. The condition of the heart and the residency of the Holy Spirit will be obvious by the integrity of a person's overall character.

The Gift and the Gifts

The gifts of the Spirit are quite different from the fruit of the Spirit. While the fruit is to be the normal display of God's presence at work in all believers, the gifts are specific endowments for service that are given on an individual basis. There is also an essential difference between the gift (singular) of the Holy Spirit and the gifts (plural) of the Holy Spirit.

The Holy Spirit himself is the gift of God (singular) to all believers. When the Spirit was first poured out on the New Testament church, Peter preached to the onlookers: "Repent and be baptized, every one of you, in the name of Jesus Christ for the forgiveness of your sins. And you will receive the gift of the Holy Spirit" (Acts 2:38). Later, when Peter preached at the house of Cornelius in Caesarea; "the Holy Spirit came on all who heard the message. The circumcised believers who had come with Peter were astonished that the gift of the Holy Spirit had been poured out even on the Gentiles" (Acts 10:44-45). It is the Holy Spirit who convicts of sin, draws people to Christ, transforms them through the New Birth, and bears witness of their acceptance before God. He is the One who teaches through reading and meditating on the scriptures. He is the One who comforts the grieving, guides the lost, and lights the way when the path seems unclear. It is the Holy Spirit who intercedes with the Father, empowers for service, and enables perseverance to the end. Therefore, it is he who is to be the focus of the believer's desire, not the gifts that he may confer.

That does not mean that the gifts of the Spirit are unimportant. They are vital to the overall health of the community of believers. These gifts are bestowed for specific purposes of service. They are never for the benefit of the person receiving them, but always for the good of others. The Spirit does not bless us through the gifts he gives us; rather he blesses us through the gifts he gives to those around us who use their gifts to minister to us. Spiritual gifts are not for admiration or ego or emotion or ambition. They are never to be envied and cannot be self-generated. When the Holy Spirit comes, he grants certain gifts of his own choosing according to his purpose for the good of the corporate body of believers and the building of God's Kingdom. The blessing is not in obtaining spiritual gifts; the blessing is in using spiritual gifts for their intended purpose.

Unlike the fruit of the Spirit, which is clearly defined in a single scriptural passage, the gifts of the Spirits are spoken of less precisely and in a variety of scriptural passages. Romans 12:6-8; 1 Corinthians 12:7-11, 28-30; Ephesians 4:11-12; and 1 Peter 4:10-11, provide the primary references to spiritual gifts. The overall biblical approach to the topic makes it quite apparent that there is no intent to provide a comprehensive list of all possible gifts. The gifts are not neatly packaged products that can be easily cataloged and analyzed. This somewhat indefinable aspect of the spiritual gifts further highlights the fact that the Spirit himself is the focal point, not the individual gifts.

Wesley actually had very little to say about the gifts of the Holy Spirit. This is largely because he considered most of them to have passed away after the first few centuries of the church. However, he did not attribute this cessation to the will of God, but to the lack of genuine Christianity within the church.

> We seldom hear of them after that fatal period when the Emperor Constantine called himself a Christian; and, from a vain imagination of promoting the Christian cause thereby, heaped riches and power and honour upon the Christians in general, but in particular upon the Christian Clergy. From this time they almost totally ceased; very few instances of the kind where found. The cause of this was not, (as has been vulgarly supposed) "because there was no more occasion for them.". . .The real cause was, "the love of many," almost all Christians, so called, was "waxed cold." The Christians had no more of the Spirit of Christ than the other Heathens. . . .This was the real reason why the extraordinary gifts of the Holy Ghost were no longer to be found in the Christian Church; because the Christians were turned Heathen again, and had only a dead form left.[6]

But there is a further, more practical, reason why Wesley was not overly concerned with spiritual gifts. His attention was given more to the fruit of the Spirit as the most convincing evidence of God's presence and work in a person's life. He believed in the spiritual gifts, but he kept them in proper perspective. This outlook remains generally representative of most contemporary Wesleyans. It is an attitude of openness to and appreciation for the gifts, but with greater emphasis on the daily fruit of the Spirit as the ultimate expression of authentic holiness.

---

[6]   *Works* 7:26–27.

Spiritual Formation in the Holy Life

Wesleyan Spirituality

Spiritual formation, or Christian spirituality, is the contemporary term used to describe the process of spiritual growth that informs and guides an intimate walk with God. Spirituality is a fashionable word in the modern climate of religious pluralism. The Druid rituals of nature worship, claims of alien abduction, and even acts of terrorism are described in terms of spirituality. This generic concept of spirituality refers to virtually any experience that a person deems to be meaningful. But Christian spirituality is a much more specific term. As Oxford theologian Alister McGrath explains: "For Christianity, spirituality concerns the living out of the encounter with Jesus Christ. . . . Christian spirituality may be thus understood as the way in which Christian individuals or groups aim to deepen their experience of God."[7] In other words, spiritual formation is the process whereby believers nurture their relationship with Christ. Through such means as prayer, scripture reading, and worship they seek to follow him more closely and to grow in his image. Ultimately, spiritual formation is about growth in holiness. Not growth *into* holiness, but growth *within* holiness.

The different Christian traditions have taken somewhat different approaches to spiritual formation. The focus of Catholic spirituality is the liturgy of worship. The sacrament of the Mass is held in especially high regard because it is believed to make the body and blood of Christ literally present in the believer. Mary and the saints also play a key role in Catholic spirituality as they intercede for both the living and the dead. Eastern Orthodox spirituality is rooted in the traditions of the early church. This includes the theological and devotional writings of significant thinkers in the first few centuries of the church. Icons play an important role. These are not idols or objects of worship, but pictures and images of Christ and the saints that are used to aid worshippers in glimpsing the mystery and reality of divine truth. The "Jesus Prayer" ("Lord Jesus Christ, Son of God, have mercy on me") is also a frequent feature in worship. Unlike Catholicism and Orthodoxy, Protestant spirituality looks directly to the Bible rather than liturgical forms. Scripture reading and prayer are central to Protestantism. The emphasis is on the cross of Christ, personal conversion, and intimate fellowship with God through the ministry of the Holy Spirit.[8]

---

[7] Alister E. McGrath, *Christian Spirituality: An Introduction* (Oxford: Blackwell, 1999) 2–3.

[8] Ibid., 14–17.

Spirituality within the Wesleyan context is not fundamentally different from that of other Christian traditions. It shares the same common core of beliefs and values. Naturally, it contains the general character of Protestant spirituality. There is strong emphasis on the cross, personal conversion, scripture reading, prayer, and corporate worship. Wesleyan spirituality does, however, take on some distinctive aspects that reflect Wesley's original influence. These include the significance of the Lord's Supper, mutual support and accountability, self-discipline, and service to others.

The key to understanding Wesleyan spirituality is to understand that entire sanctification is not the end, but the beginning of authentic Christianity. This is the primary difference between Wesleyan spirituality and the spirituality of other traditions. Most traditions see spiritual formation as the pursuit of holiness. But Wesleyan theology sees it the other way around. Holiness does not grow out of spiritual formation; holiness produces spiritual formation. Therefore, holiness is not the elusive end result for a saintly few, but the foundational experience of all believers that nourishes and supports the growth of spiritual vitality.

The Grand Channel of Communion

Baptism and the Lord's Supper are the two sacraments generally recognized by all Protestants. "Sacrament" is not a term found in the Bible. It comes from a Latin word that signified an oath of allegiance. The Christian usage of the word came to refer to certain rituals that are performed in the belief that God uses them to bring special grace to the believer. They are not viewed as magical rites, but as means of grace. They are described as the outward visible signs of the inward spiritual grace that is received from God. The Catholic tradition recognizes seven sacraments: baptism, the Lord's Supper, confirmation, penance, extreme unction (anointing in preparation for death), ordination, and marriage. Protestantism recognizes only baptism and the Lord's Supper because they are the only two actually instituted by Christ. The Lord's Supper is highlighted here because of its importance in the theology and experience of Wesley.

Wesley took the Lord's Prayer reference to "our daily bread" in a very literal sense. In his "Sermon on the Mount—VI," he cites the early church as providing historical precedence for the idea that communion should be taken daily. Although he did not actually press the point to insist on this, it was his personal practice to participate in the Lord's Supper at least once a week. By no means was this merely a ritualistic habit of an overly zealous man. Communion was essential to Wesley's understanding of Christian faith and practice. He viewed it as "the grand channel whereby the grace of his Spirit was conveyed to the souls of all the children of God."[9]

Historically there have been four predominant ways of thinking on how the Lord's Supper invokes the presence of Jesus. The oldest idea comes from the Orthodox and Catholic traditions. It is the belief that the elements of bread and wine actually become the body and blood of Jesus when properly consecrated and received. The key feature in this doctrine is the belief that Jesus literally becomes physically present in the sacrament. Next came the doctrine taught by Martin Luther. Luther was not quite as rigid in his understanding of Christ's presence. He believed Jesus is literally present in the elements themselves, but not that the elements actually became the body and blood of Jesus. John Calvin stepped yet farther away from a literal understanding of Christ's presence. He held that Jesus is truly present in the sacrament, but not in any bodily sense at all. His presence is purely spiritual. Another reformer, Ulrich Zwingli, proposed the least literal view of Christ's presence in the Lord's Supper. He saw communion purely as an act of remembrance. He believed Christ is present, but not in any sense that is unusual or particularly significant. The sacrament is a symbolic time to affirm faith, contemplate the meaning of Christ's sacrifice, and give thanks.

Wesley incorporated the key features of both Calvin and Zwingli. Like Zwingli, he understood the Lord's Supper to be a memorial or commemoration of Christ's death. But like Calvin, he also understood that Christ is uniquely present in the Supper in a way that cannot be experienced otherwise. In the act of communion believers receive a particularly healing and strengthening measure of grace. This is why Wesley referred to the Lord's Supper as the "grand channel" of God's grace, why he valued its role so highly and why he received it as often as possible.

Modern Wesleyans have often failed to value this sacrament in the way Wesley did. Most have adopted the thought of Zwingli and regarded it merely as a ritual of remembrance. Because of this, it is only occasionally observed in some churches, rarely in others, and not at all in a few. An absence of the mystery of grace results in a devaluation of the sacrament itself. As a devalued sacrament, it comes to be seen as a respectable, but fundamentally meaningless, practice from ancient times. It may even be considered irrelevant to contemporary Christianity.

The authentic Wesleyan understanding of communion recognizes that Christ is uniquely present at the Supper and that participants are uniquely blessed by his presence. It is the Lord's Supper not because it is a remembrance that he was once here. It is the Lord's Supper because he is the present

9   *Works* 5:338.

host who invites *his* guests to *his* feast and who joins with them in the fellowship of *his* table.

Wesley also held another view of communion that is largely overlooked by modern Wesleyans. He believed the grace that comes through the sacrament is not just a grace of blessing, but a grace of conviction. Like most other Protestants, those Wesleyans who do take the sacrament seriously tend to place great emphasis on the need for the participant to be wholly right with God before approaching the table. Therefore, only committed Christians are invited to participate, at least by implication. This comes mainly from a misunderstanding of Paul's warning against partaking of the sacrament "in an unworthy manner" (1 Corinthians 11:27). But Wesley believed a person could come to the table a sinner and leave the table a converted Christian. Of course, he was speaking of one who comes in a sincere attitude of sorrow for sin and searching for God.

Like many of Wesley's understandings, this too is rooted in both scripture and experience. Scripturally, he cites the fact of the first Lord's Supper: "Our Lord commanded those very men who were then unconverted, who had not received the Holy Ghost, who (in the full sense of the word) were not believers, to do this 'in remembrance of' him. Here the precept is clear. And to these he delivered the elements with his own hands."[10] Experientially, Wesley cites the cases of many he knew personally. "Ye are the witnesses. For many now present know, the very beginning of your conversion to God (perhaps, in some, the first deep conviction) was wrought at the Lord's Supper."[11] For Wesley, the Lord's Supper could serve the same purpose as an evangelistic altar call. This, too, has been lost in much of modern Wesleyanism.

The Role of Spiritual Disciplines

Wesley is often remembered for the self-discipline that characterized so much of his life. He was, however, neither the first nor the last to see the importance of discipline in spiritual formation. More recently, Richard Foster's *Celebration of Discipline* has been recognized as a modern classic in the field of Christian spirituality. Foster classifies the spiritual disciplines into categories of inward disciplines (meditation, prayer, fasting, study), outward disciplines (simplicity, solitude, submission, service), and corporate disciplines (confession, worship, guidance, celebration).

Perhaps the key to understanding the significance of the spiritual disciplines is to understand what they are intended to do and who is intended to practice them. As to their purpose, Foster states simply that "The classical

---

[10]   *Works* 1:279–80.

[11]   Ibid., 279.

Disciplines of the spiritual life call us to move beyond surface living into the depths."[12] As to who is intended to practice them, he elaborates more fully.

> We must not be led to believe that the Disciplines are only for spiritual giants and hence beyond our reach, or only for contemplatives who devote their time to prayer and meditation. Far from it. God intends the Disciplines of the spiritual life to be for ordinary human beings: people who have jobs, who care for children, who wash dishes and mow lawns. In fact, the Disciplines are best exercised in the midst of our relationships with our husband or wife, our brothers and sisters, our friends and neighbors.[13]

In other words, the spiritual disciplines are like all other tools of spiritual formation; they are for everyone. They do not make Christians holy; they take them deeper into holiness. This is certainly in keeping with the Wesleyan concept of growth within holiness. Although Wesley did not formally systematize the disciplines as Foster has done, he certainly practiced and taught them in one way or another.

The point here is to emphasize the close relationship between the Wesleyan concept of holiness and the age old concern for spiritual formation. It has been said that the Wesleyan teaching of holiness and the classic concept of spiritual formation "have so much in common that a marriage is in order. Their compatibility centers in their mutual concern for holy living. For both, the standard is Christ-likeness. There can be no other meaningful measurement for spiritual formation or sanctified living."[14]

———•———

Wesley abhorred any appearance of hypocrisy, self-righteousness, or spiritual pride. That is why he insisted that the true expression of authentic holiness was always a matter of Spirit-filled character rather than pious talk or religious exercise. Although he placed great importance on how the Christian life is lived, his first concern was the condition of the heart. That same focus remains paramount in Wesleyan theology. Some strands of the movement have strayed down the path of legalism; others have pursued the illusion of cultural relativism and theological diversity. But the real essence of authentic Christian expression in the Wesleyan tradition remains the Spirit-filled lives of real people in the real world.

---

[12] Richard J. Foster, *Celebration of Discipline: The Path to Spiritual Growth*, 20th Anniversary ed. (New York: Harper Collins, 1998) 1.

[13] Ibid.

[14] Wesley D. Tracy, E. Dee Freeborn, Janine Tartaglia, and Morris A. Weigelt, *The Upward Call: Spiritual Formation and the Holy Life* (Kansas City: Beacon Hill, 1994) 9.

13

The Responsibility of Holiness

Holiness and Christian Ethics

The Nature of Christian Ethics

AUTHENTIC HOLINESS is an ethical holiness. It is a holiness that moves beyond the level of private spiritual experience into the realm of interaction with the real world. Ethics is the branch of philosophy that deals with issues of right and wrong. In the opening paragraph of his classic book titled *Ethics*, Dietrich Bonhoeffer stated that "The knowledge of good and evil seems to be the aim of all ethical reflection. The first task of Christian ethics is to invalidate this knowledge."[1] Bonhoeffer's point is that the world's perception of good and evil is inaccurate. It is flawed because the world itself is fallen and corrupted. Therefore, it cannot discern real good from real evil. Since God alone has true knowledge of good and evil, we can only begin to grasp the true meaning of those concepts by viewing them from God's perspective. This is the work of Christian ethics.

Christians seek to view the world through the biblical lens. This means they approach ethical issues from a completely different viewpoint than non-Christians. They take into account that humanity was originally created in God's image of holiness, that humanity fell from holiness into sin, and that the entire world has been ravaged by the evils of sin ever since. But they also recognize that God has not abandoned his lost creation. There is a Savior who has come to restore all things to God. Therefore, their ethical response to the world's problems reflects those basic beliefs. Christian ethics seeks solutions founded on God's saving act of redemption in Jesus Christ rather than solutions founded on a misguided notion of human goodness.

---

[1] Dietrich Bonhoeffer, *Ethics*, ed. Eberhard Bethge (New York: Macmillan, 1979) 17.

Discussions of ethics normally use the abstract language of theory and scholarship. In reality ethics is an intensely practical field of study. This is because it deals with the things we actually do on a day to day basis. It guides and informs the link between beliefs, values, and behavior. This is especially true in Christian ethics, where the integrity of the faith itself is at stake. The issue is not moralistic rules and regulations. The issue is how the Christian's profession of faith and code of conduct actually interact. In other words, is there continuity and consistency—the two ingredients necessary to integrity? Jesus got to the heart of the matter with a very simple image: "Make a tree good and its fruit will be good, or make a tree bad and its fruit will be bad, for a tree is recognized by its fruit" (Matthew 12:33). James picked up the same theme when he asked, "Can both fresh water and salt water flow from the same spring? My brothers, can a fig tree bear olives, or a grapevine bear figs? Neither can a salt spring produce fresh water" (James 3:11-12). This is the concern of the ethics of holiness. A holiness that preaches figs but bears olives is not authentic. A holiness that preaches behavior but omits change of heart is not authentic. A holiness that preaches perfect love but fails to fulfill its moral duty to society is not authentic.

The Holiness Ethic of Love

It is impossible to read the Bible and reasonably conclude that salvation is a purely private affair between God and the individual self. The social dimension of God's plan for humanity is evident from beginning to end. God's first order of business in the Garden of Eden was to respond to his own analysis that, "It is not good for the man to be alone. I will make a helper suitable for him" (Genesis 2:18). Likewise, one of the last images in the Bible is that of "a great multitude that no one could count, from every nation, tribe, people and language standing before the throne and in front of the Lamb" (Revelation 7:9). In between are hundreds of references to the theme of human interaction and the corresponding responsibilities that God places on people in those interactions. In other words, one's relationship with God affects and involves others.

But what is the standard by which the ethical dimension of this interaction is judged? A common assumption today is that there is no actual standard. Ethical relativism is the widely accepted notion that right and wrong cannot be spoken of in absolute terms. Right and wrong are merely fluid categories of subjective judgment that conform to changing opinions. What is right or wrong for one person is not necessarily right or wrong for another person. Joseph Fletcher popularized this viewpoint in the 1960s with his publication of *Situation Ethics*. He allowed for only one absolute: "Only one 'thing' is intrinsically good; namely, love: nothing else at all."[2]

On the surface Fletcher's ethic of love may sound very Christian. His concept of love, however, is not the biblical concept. When carried out to its logical conclusion, as Fletcher does, it becomes absurdly unchristian and unbiblical. In Fletcher's ethic, everything is relative. "Therefore what is sometimes good may at other times be evil, and what is sometimes wrong, may sometimes be right when it serves a good enough end—*depending on the situation*."[3] His eventual conclusion is that, "We cannot say anything we do *is* good, only that it is a means to an end and therefore *happens* in that cause-and-effect relation to have value."[4]

Fletcher's ethic was essentially repeated a few years later by Anglican bishop John A. T. Robinson in *Christian Freedom in a Permissive Society*. But Robinson's position virtually removed the concept of situation ethics from the Christian context in which Fletcher had attempted to develop it. Robinson declared that there is a "dimension of reality which causes men to create God." According to Robinson, people no longer need to think of God in any traditional or biblical sense. He says, "the theist mold has been shattered. The shaping of the stuff of that experience into a God existing as a Being, in another realm, above or beyond this one, is no longer credible."[5] The foundational work of Fletcher and Robinson continues to express the essence of the ethic of humanistic relativism.

The Christian ethic takes a far different view. Having love as the ultimate goal does not justify every means. In Fletcher's ethic no action is ever wrong if the person carrying out the action claims love as the motive. The ethic of holiness is also an ethic of love, but love of an entirely different kind. The ethic of holiness embodies, reflects, and points to the love of God in Christ. It recognizes the realities of a fallen world. It builds its values on the power of God's grace and the faithfulness of his love. And it interacts with the world in light of those values of holiness. Just as the theological definition of holiness is to love God with all our heart, soul, mind, and strength; so the ethical definition of holiness is to love our neighbor as ourselves.

The premier Wesleyan–Holiness theologian of a past generation, H. Orton Wiley, described this ethic of love as "the duties we owe to others."[6]

---

2   Joseph Fletcher, *Situation Ethics: The New Morality* (Philadelphia: Westminster, 1966) 57.

3   Ibid., 123.

4   Ibid., 129.

5   John A. T. Robinson, *Christian Freedom in a Permissive Society* (Philadelphia: Westminster, 1970) 131.

6   H. Orton Wiley, *Christian Theology*, 3 vols. (Kansas City: Beacon Hill, 1940–43) 3:68–69.

He said the first Christian duty is to love all people with the love of good will. Christians are never to wish misfortune or harm toward anyone. Instead, they are to actively pursue good on behalf of others in every reasonable way possible. Jesus stated the essence of this duty in the Golden Rule: "So in everything, do to others what you would have them do to you, for this sums up the Law and the Prophets" (Matthew 7:12). Furthermore, Christians are to love those in need with the love of compassion. Even if the one in need is an enemy, he is to receive the ethic of love. "If your enemy is hungry, feed him; if he is thirsty, give him something to drink. In doing this you will heap burning coals on his head" (Romans 12:20). The purpose of the burning coals of love is not to cause harm, but to overcome evil with good. And finally, followers of Christ are to love good people with the love of complacency. By this Wiley seems to mean the satisfaction or completeness that should naturally exist among believers. It is the fulfillment of the new command that Jesus gave his followers: "As I have loved you, so you must love one another. By this all men will know that you are my disciples" (John13:34-35).

This is holiness ethics at work in the lives of believers. It is an ethic in which people demonstrate the integrity of the gospel at a personal level through their public dealings and their private relationships. But the ethic of holiness is not only personal, it also profoundly social. It deals responsibly with society as a whole.

Holiness and Social Action

A Wesleyan Social Ethic

For John Wesley the link between holiness and social ethics was always obvious. He insisted that "the gospel of Christ knows no religion, but social; no holiness but social holiness."[7] He was not denying the personal dimension of religion and holiness, but was merely affirming that Christians do not live in a vacuum. They are part of a particular culture and community. They are in the world even though they are not of the world. While here they are morally obligated to be salt and light to the world. That is, to be a positive influence. Christians are to be a blessing to fallen society, not a burden. This does not mean they will be popular or even appreciated. In fact, Jesus said they would be hated by the world. Regardless of that, they are to obey the commands and follow the examples of Jesus in their dealings with society.

As briefly described in earlier chapters, Wesley's sense of social responsibility was immense. Throughout his entire adult life he was actively involved

---

[7] *Works* 14:321.

in compassionate ministries to prisoners, orphans, widows, the uneducated, the unemployed, and the sick. He referred to these and other such deeds as "works of mercy." They included, "The feeding the hungry, the clothing the naked, the entertaining or assisting the stranger, the visiting those that are sick or in prison, the comforting the afflicted, the instructing the ignorant, the reproving the wicked, the exhorting and encouraging the well-doer."[8]

It is obvious that Wesley's understanding of social holiness went far beyond merely praying for the needy and giving money to charities. He saw that true social holiness is personal, as his journal entry for November 24, 1760, reveals.

> I visited as many as I could of the sick. How much better it is, when it can be done, to *carry* relief to the poor, than to *send* it! And that both for our own sake and theirs. For *theirs*, as it is so much more comfortable to them, and as we may assist them in spirituals as well as temporals; and for *our own*, as it is far more apt to soften our heart, and to make us naturally care for each other.[9]

Wesley continued to echo this theme in his sermon, "On Visiting the Sick." When speaking of the needy and afflicted he asks: "But is there need of visiting them in person? May we not relieve them at a distance? Does it not answer the same purpose if we send them help, as if we carry it ourselves?" To which he responds emphatically that when direct contact with the needy is avoided, "you could not gain that increase in lowliness, in patience, in tenderness of spirit, in sympathy with the afflicted, which you might have gained, if you had visited them in person."[10]

Finally, it should be observed that Wesley practiced what he preached. In January 1785, at the age of eighty-one, he spend five days on the streets of London begging for money to buy clothes for the poor: "I walked through the town, and begged two hundred pounds, in order to clothe them that needed it most. But it was hard work, as most of the streets were filled with melting snow, which often lay ankle deep: so that my feet were steeped in snow water nearly from morning till evening."[11] He only stopped when forced by illness after the fifth day.

The priority of social ethics is self-evident within Wesley's concept of holiness. He understood and lived out the biblical concept of holiness that is both personal *and* social. Unfortunately, many of his spiritual descendents have failed to make that connection; opting either for a personal experience

---

8   *Works* 5:329.
9   *Works* 3:28.
10   *Works* 7:119–20.
11   *Works* 4:295.

that focuses solely on the needs and feelings of the self, or pursuing a humanistic social gospel that often has more concern for political agenda than grace, faith, and salvation.

So what does an authentic social ethic look like that is true to scripture and consistent with the Wesleyan spirit? Ronald Stone's outline of Wesley's ethical model serves as a helpful guide.[12]

Human freedom. Wesley had a profound respect for God's gift of human freedom. This was not only a theological doctrine; it was also an ethical imperative. He believed passionately in the human right to freedom. This was demonstrated most obviously in his opposition to slavery, but it was also essential to his other social concerns. He wanted to help people become free from the dark sides of society that trapped them in poverty, abuse, crime, and disease.

The life of love. Holiness is love for God and love for others. Wesley's early social ethic was predominately motivated by his effort to achieve personal holiness through social action. After Aldersgate his social ethic became an ethic of love. He loved humanity and he loved individuals. Wesley could never be accused of operating from a sentimental or emotional view of love. His ethic of love was grounded in the love of God. It was a love that pursued the well-being of others.

Realism. Wesley was not naïve. He was well acquainted with the harsh realities and the sinful condition of those he sought to love and help. He understood from the life of Jesus and his own experiences that people often reject those who seek to help them. He also understood that there are cultural and environmental limitations to what can be done for others.

Natural law. This refers to reason, logic, and the intuitive sense of fundamental right and wrong that remains in the human race in spite of its fallen condition. In other words, Wesley did not claim God as his authority in every social opinion. He read widely in social science, political theory, history, philosophy, and law. He used this knowledge to reflect on the problems of society and the appropriate ways to respond to those problems.

Scripture. Although Wesley utilized outside sources for information and guidance, everything was ultimately filtered through the truth of the Bible. He did not blindly accept everything he read from secular literature, but neither did he reject it just because it was secular. Rather, he put it to the test of scripture. What passed the test was useable; what failed the test was not useable. But the Bible was more than just a sieve for straining out unacceptable ideas. It was the normative guide for everything he did. Christ is the model of love in action, and therefore, his example is to be followed and obeyed.

---

[12] Ronald H. Stone, *John Wesley's Life and Ethics* (Nashville: Abingdon, 2001) 208–10.

Tradition. The beliefs and practices of the early church are highly revered in the Wesleyan tradition. The New Testament church in Acts and the first few centuries of the developing Christian community are particularly significant. For example, the anonymous author of *A Letter to Diognetus* wrote the following observations of Christians in the second century.

> Christians cannot be distinguished from the rest of the human race by country or language or customs. They do not live in cities of their own; they do not use a peculiar form of speech; they do not follow an eccentric manner of life. . . .They follow the customs of their country in clothing and food and other matters of daily living. . .but only as aliens. They marry like everyone else, and beget their children, but do not cast out their offspring. They share their board with each other but not their marriage bed. They obey the established laws, but in their own lives they go far beyond what the law requires. They love all men, and by all men are persecuted. They are poor and yet they make many rich; they are completely destitute, yet they enjoy abundance.[13]

This was the very model of social ethics and witness that Wesley sought to fulfill in his own life and in the lives of those who called themselves Methodists.

Experience. It has been noted in earlier chapters that Wesley allowed experience to influence his theology and his practice of ministry. He taught entire sanctification not just because he believed it was biblical, but also because of the testimonies of people who had experienced it. He was first convinced of the truth of assurance of salvation by the experience of the Moravians in the terror of an ocean storm. Likewise, he later endorsed the ministry of lay preachers (both men and women) because experience proved them to be anointed and used by God.

The influence of real life experience in the Wesleyan social ethic reflects the practical nature of Wesleyanism as a whole. The holiness ethic of social interaction may thus be summarized as an ethic of sanctified love, Christ-like compassion, and Wesleyan pragmatism.

Evangelism as Social Responsibility

The ethical aspect of holiness is intricately entwined with the whole of Christian experience. This means that ethical considerations impact all facets of the spiritual life. Evangelism is one such place. Evangelism is usually asso-

---

[13] Carl A. Volz, *Faith and Practice in the Early Church: Foundations for Contemporary Theology* (Minneapolis: Augsburg, 1983) 177–78.

ciated with saving souls and preparing people for heaven. There are, however, ethical implications for evangelism.

From the Christian perspective evangelism itself is a form of social responsibility. Wesley certainly understood that evangelism is not just a matter of salvation for individuals. Evangelism benefits the whole of society. The very history of eighteenth century Britain demonstrates that a society touched by a tide of genuine spiritual renewal is a society that improves at all levels. In Wesley's lifetime he witnessed the effects of thousands of citizens coming to Christ in a relatively short time. As old values were transformed into new biblical values, people found their quality of life improving. They became honest workers, learned to read, saved money, and raised stable families. The impact on society, especially in the local communities most touched by the revival, was significant.

Within the task of evangelism there are several ethical responsibilities. The first responsibility is to ensure that salvation is not equated with escapism. Skeptics sometimes criticize the entire concept of evangelism on the grounds that it is nothing more than a numbing drug for hurting people. People are more likely to turn to Christ when they are troubled or in trouble. Their search for salvation, say the critics, merely reflects their longing to escape the hard realities of life. What better way to avoid problems here than by simply ignoring them while looking to a highly personalized hereafter? The ethical dimension of evangelism demands that salvation be communicated to the lost in terms of its present realities as well as its future hope. In other words, coming to Christ is not an evasion of personal accountability.

Second is the ethical responsibility of portraying present realities with honest candor. It is one thing to promise Christ's strength and help to a troubled seeker; but it is something else to promise that if they turn to Jesus their troubles will disappear and happiness will flow. Christ certainly does transform the derelict and heal the brokenhearted. But that does not mean the emotional scares of the abused will simply melt away or that a shattered marriage will suddenly become bliss. An ethical evangelism may truthfully point to the Savior as the healer of broken emotions and marriages. An ethical evangelism cannot, however, dole out exaggerated promises anymore than it can sell indulgences for sin.

Third, evangelism must not foster elitism. While it is true that all believers are no longer to be of the world, they must continue to face the fact that they are still in the world. The church is not a fortress; it is a family, and families live in and interact with their communities as a whole. Believers who properly represent the family of God do not remain aloof from their neighbors or flaunt moral self-righteousness. They simply live the faith among their neighbors and respond in obedience as the Holy Spirit opens doors of opportunity for witness and ministry.

The fourth ethical responsibility of evangelism speaks to the church itself. It addresses the family of God as a family. As David Bosch states it, "Believers cannot accept one another as members of a community of faith without this having consequences for their day-to-day life and for the world."[14] His point is primarily a reference to unity within the church. When evangelism occurs and converts are brought into the community of faith, everyone must be taught and reminded of the ethical responsibilities that are owed to one another. Believers are to love one another not just because it makes for a positive witness to the world (which it does), but first and foremost because it is the single most fundamental command of Christ. If Christians cannot love each other and deal with each other in ethically responsible ways, what hope is there for how they will deal with the rest of the world?

There is yet a further dimension to the ethics of evangelism that all Christians must face. In contemporary terminology it is called the question of contextualization. This is a much debated topic in the current literature of evangelism and cross-cultural missions. Simply stated, it is the question of how far Christians should go in accommodating themselves to their surrounding culture in order to evangelize within that culture. Although the dispute between Paul and Peter in Galatians 2:11-21 is not exactly about contextualization, it illustrates the sensitivities that are at stake. Peter had adopted the practice of eating with Gentiles. But when pressured by a group of Jews, he withdrew from his overt association with the Gentiles. Paul accused Peter of hypocrisy because of his double standard and lack of consist adherence to what he had really come to believe.

The point of the controversy in this incident was the relationship between Christian faith and social culture. How much of what is perceived to be fundamentally Christian is in fact culturally determined? Wesley and Whitefield were severely criticized for taking the gospel out of the church and into the fields. Wesley's openness to this form of contextualization did not come easily. By his own admission, "I should have thought the saving of souls almost a sin, if it had not been done in a church."[15] A century later, in his efforts to evangelize the Chinese, Hudson Taylor was virtually shunned by fellow Christians because he adopted Chinese dress and lived in the Chinese community rather than a mission compound. Of course the historical precedent goes back much further. Jesus himself was despised by the religious

---

[14] David J. Bosch, *Transforming Mission: Paradigm Shifts in Theology of Mission* (Maryknoll, N.Y.: Orbis, 1998) 151.

[15] *Works* 1:120.

elite of his culture for entering, and apparently enjoying, the company of sinners.

Today the issues continue to multiply as more and more countries are reached with the gospel by missionaries. For example, one of the most common dilemmas faced by Christians and missionaries in some countries is the practice of bribery. Many cultures view bribery as simply a necessary and accepted way of life. But in most Western cultures bribery is not only considered immoral, it is illegal. Bribery presents just one example of the multitude of ethical dilemmas faced by Christians in every part of the world. It highlights the fact that the culturally accepted lines of evangelistic contextualization are drawn differently in Kansas than in Germany or Brazil.

So how does one know where to draw the line? Perhaps the model of Wesley's social ethic can help. Does the proposed action respect the fundamental human rights of freedom and dignity? Does it reflect the love of God and the love of Christians? Is it realistic in its approach and expected outcome? Is it reasonable in these same regards? Is there any historical precedence from the early church that sheds light on the issue? What has been the experience of others in similar situations? And most importantly, what does the Bible say? Is it in violation of any scriptural commands or values? Is there an example from the life of Jesus or the apostles that reveals a guiding principle for such cases?

The Christian faith is an ethical faith. It seeks to fulfill the biblical law of love and integrity in everyday life. This ethic of holiness recognizes that practical demonstrations of Christian compassion are inseparable from authentic Christian faith. Through prayers, good deeds, and acts of mercy the love of Christ is spread throughout society. But the ethic of holiness also recognizes that the renewal of society is not accomplished by such efforts. These are only salt and light, they are not transformation. Societal transformation comes only by the direct power of God's saving grace in the lives of the individuals who make up a society. And that saving grace is made known most effectively through the evangelistic efforts of Spirit-filled believers.

14

Questions along the Way

WESLEY MADE frequent use of the question/answer format in his teaching on Christian holiness. These were compiled and included in his classic work, *A Plain Account of Christian Perfection*. He found this method to be an effective means of addressing specific points that were of greatest concern to many people. Some contemporary Wesleyan writers have utilized Wesley's model by creating their own versions of his question/answer format.[1] This final chapter draws from these and other sources to assemble a summarizing collection of some of the most common questions that emerge. They are divided into the two categories of doctrine and experience.

Questions on Holiness Doctrine

1. What is the difference between holiness, entire sanctification, and perfection?

Although these terms are often used interchangeably, there are, technically speaking, differences between them. Holiness is a very broad term that signifies moral purity. It is the absence of sin. In its truest sense it can only be used in reference to God, for holiness is the essential character of God. However, the Bible also indicates that God makes things and people holy when he purifies them for his purpose. The simplest definition of holiness as it relates to people is Christ-likeness.

Entire sanctification refers to the work of God in the heart of a Christian that makes the person holy. In this work God purifies the Christian's heart from its natural inclination toward sin. It is called entire sanctification to distinguish it from the related concepts of initial sanctification (Christian conversion) and progressive sanctification (spiritual growth).

---

[1] For example see Keith W. Drury, *Holiness for Ordinary People* (Indianapolis: Wesleyan Publishing House, 1993); and J. Kenneth Grider, *Entire Sanctification* (Kansas City: Beacon Hill, 1980).

Perfection is one of the consequences of entire sanctification. It is better to use the expression "perfection of love." Perfection by itself implies many things that are not included in the biblical idea of perfection of love. The perfection of the Christian's love for God is the fulfillment of Jesus' command to love God with the whole heart, mind, soul, and strength.

In summary, holiness is the quality of Christ-likeness; entire sanctification is the work of God that makes one Christ-like; and perfection of love is the resulting relationship with God that follows entire sanctification.

2. Is perfection of love a real experience or just an ideal goal to work toward?

Perfect love is a real experience for this life. It is not merely an idealized goal of growth. It is a gift from God that is received by faith, much in the same way that salvation is received by faith. The biblical directives to be perfect refer to a completed action in the present life. It must be remembered that no one makes himself perfect in his love for God. This is something God does within believers.

3. Why is entire sanctification called a second work of grace?

The "secondness" of entire sanctification refers to the fact that it is a work of God's grace that is separate from, and follows after, the experience of conversion. The two experiences are different because they deal with the two different types of sin. At conversion God forgives sins that have actually been committed. At entire sanctification God deals with the inherent inclination toward sin that all humans are born with due to Adam's fall.

4. Why is entire sanctification called a cleansing experience?

This is because of the way God deals with the problem of inherent, or original, sin. This sin does not require God's forgiveness, for it is not sin that has actually been committed. God does not hold people accountable for the fallen condition they have inherited. But still, the presence of this sin in the human heart needs to be dealt with. The Bible speaks of this as a cleansing or purifying act of God in the heart.

5. Why is entire sanctification called an instantaneous work of grace?

It is instantaneous in the sense that there is a specific point in time at which this work of God's grace occurs. For some people it is a very obvious, perhaps even dramatic, spiritual event that is easily identified. For others it may be much more subtle and less apparent. But even in this case, there is still a moment in time when it happens even though the process leading up to it may be fairly gradual. Thus, it is still instantaneous. Wesley compared this type of experience to a very slow death. Although the process of death may be very gradual, there is still a distinct point at which the person passes from this life to the next.

6. Is entire sanctification the same thing as being filled with the Holy Spirit?

Technically speaking, they are not the same thing, though they are closely associated. Entire sanctification is the purifying and perfecting act of God in the believer's heart. The fullness of the Holy Spirit accompanies that act. Some like to think of it as the Holy Spirit moving into the void created by the purging of the sinful nature. So the two events are virtually simultaneous in occurrence, but by definition they are actually two distinct events.

The problem with using these two expressions interchangeably is the resulting implication that the Holy Spirit has been previously absent from the believer. In fact, the presence of the Holy Spirit is received at conversion. It is he who draws people to Christ, convicts them of their need for Christ, and leads them in the initial steps of walking with Christ. However, it is not until entire sanctification that the Spirit has full access to every facet of the believer's heart and life. Therefore, it is in that sense that we may speak of the infilling of the Holy Spirit as occurring at the moment of entire sanctification.

7. Is sinless perfection taught in Wesleyan doctrine?

This is strictly a matter of what definitions one has in mind when using the term. By no means does Wesleyanism teach that we can ever reach a spiritual state in this life that places us beyond the possibility of sin. Sin was always a very real possibility even for Jesus. So in that sense, Wesleyans do not teach sinless perfection. Wesleyans do, however, take seriously the numerous biblical mandates not to sin. All believers are commanded to be sinless in the sense of abandoning the habit of willful sin. They are also to be sinless in the sense of allowing God to complete his work of heart cleansing. So, in the end, it may be said that Wesleyans do believe in following the example and commands of Christ to live without sin. But it may not be said that Wesleyans teach sinless perfection in the sense of being so perfected in piety as to be unable to sin.

Questions on Holiness Experience

1. If the inherited inclination toward sin is purged away at entire sanctification how is it possible for a sanctified person to still fall back into sin?

The word "inclination" is the key to understanding this issue. Many people mistakenly think it is original sin that causes acts of sin. This view naturally leads to the conclusion that if this inherited sin is removed then the cause of sin is removed. But original sin is not the cause of sinful actions. Adam and Eve had no original sin, yet they still committed the first sin. If original sin was the cause of acts of sins, then it would have been impossible for them to commit that sin. Likewise, Jesus had no original sin, yet it was always possible for him to commit sin, even though he did not. All of this demonstrates that sinful deeds come not from original sin itself, but from one's willful decisions to do what is wrong.

Human nature was so badly distorted by Adam's introduction of sin into the human race that all are now born with an inherently strong, and even irresistible, pull toward sin. It is this pull, or inclination, toward sin that is removed by entire sanctification. It always remains possible for the entirely sanctified to return to sin, but it is no longer inevitable that they must sin.

2. Will entire sanctification free a person from temptation?

Certainly not. Temptation is an unavoidable part of human experience, regardless of one's spiritual state. However, the entirely sanctified person does have the distinct advantage of a pure heart and the fullness of the Holy Spirit's presence to give strength in resisting temptation.

3. What happens when an entirely sanctified person does sin?

When an entirely sanctified person commits a deliberate act of sin, he literally takes a step away from God and invites the old pull toward sin back into his heart. It does not necessarily mean he has turned his back on God and abandoned his faith, but he certainly has disrupted his fellowship with God. In such cases, the Holy Spirit is faithful to bring conviction to the heart and issue a call to repentance. If the person responds in obedience there is immediate forgiveness and restoration. If the person resists the Holy Spirit and refuses to act in obedience, yet another step away from God has been taken. If this negative pattern continues, then the person has initiated the downward process commonly called backsliding. It is actually more correct to think of it as backstepping.

4. Will entire sanctification change a person's natural personality and temperament?

Generally speaking, it will not. An introvert will still be an introvert and an extrovert will still be an extrovert. A detailed person will still see details and a big picture person will still see the big picture. However, it is correct to say that after entire sanctification personality and temperament traits will be positively affected to some degree, as will every other aspect of the person's being.

5. Must people be entirely sanctified to get to heaven?

This question usually stems from the statement in Hebrews 12:14, that "without holiness no one will see the Lord." This verse is actually a part of a discussion concerning those who reject Christ. It is not a reference to those who are already walking with Christ but have not yet been entirely sanctified.

Roman Catholic doctrine teaches that original sin is cleansed at baptism and that an infant who dies prior to baptism does not gain access to heaven. (But neither do they go to hell. They are in a state of eternal limbo.) Strict Calvinism teaches that everyone is condemned to hell solely on the basis of original sin, but God has chosen to elect some to salvation. Wesleyan doctrine teaches that everyone is released from the guilt of original sin by God's sovereign act of prevenient grace. Therefore, since the blood of Christ has already covered that guilt, no one is condemned on the basis of original sin. That is why Wesleyans believe all infants who die are received into heaven, regardless of whether or not they were baptized. In other words, it is personal, deliberate acts of sin that keep people from heaven, not the inherited consequences of Adam's sin. The notion that heaven is denied to anyone who has been genuinely converted to Christ and is walking in obedience with him, but has not yet experienced entire sanctification makes a mockery of the atoning work of Jesus.

6. Why do people need to be entirely sanctified?

When the biblical concept of salvation is viewed as a whole it becomes apparent that there is more to God's plan for humanity than just the forgiveness of sin. God wants to complete his work by restoring humanity to the state of righteous and fellowship that he originally intended. In order to accomplish this restoration he must deal with the problem of sin in its total sense.

This is not merely a theoretical matter of doctrinal jargon and categories. It is an intensely practical matter of how people actually live as followers of Christ. A forgiven believer is truly transformed and born again. That must never be minimized. But, this newly born believer is very vulnerable to the attacks of Satan and the inherent pull to revert back to the old way of sin. This is why the new believer so urgently needs the care and support of the church family. But the new believer needs more than this. He needs the continuing grace and power of God to address the remaining problem of this pull back toward sin. He needs to allow God to complete his full work of salvation in entire sanctification.

This deeper experience with God will not remove all spiritual obstacles and battles. It will, however, give the sanctified believer a definite advantage in two distinct ways. First, the advantage of a new inclination of the heart that leans away from sin and toward God. And second, the advantage of a deeper and fuller experience of the Holy Spirit's presence and power.

7. Is there still room for spiritual growth after entire sanctification?

Not only is there room for growth; it is room that constantly expands. In other words, there is no completed end to spiritual growth in this life. As growth advances in one area, it reveals a myriad of new areas that need and long for nourishment and development. The process is never ending. However, this does not mean the growing Christian is always in a state of dissatisfaction. On the contrary, the growing Christian will generally enjoy a walk of inner joy and peace. The longing for more growth is not a search for meaning or fulfillment. It is rather a matter of being in an intensely loving relationship and always striving to do more to maintain and further develop that special intimacy. It is not a search for love, but an exploration of existing love. There is a great difference; a difference that can only be truly realized in the experience of growth after entire sanctification.

8. How does a person know if he or she has been entirely sanctified?

First, by the witness of the Holy Spirit. Just as the Spirit instills a sense of assurance following conversion, so he also gives a sense of assurance following entire sanctification. Attempting to describe the experience of assurance is a very difficult, and sometimes even dangerous, undertaking. That is because it is a very subjective matter that is so uniquely personal to each individual. One person's story of assurance does not necessarily fit everyone else. Those who struggle with this issue are often seeking someone else's experience that they have heard about rather than simply letting God speak to them in his own way.

Second, by the active growth and expression of the fruit of Spirit in the believer's life. This is somewhat more tangible than the witness of the Spirit. But still, caution must be exercised. On the one hand, it is easy to judge oneself too harshly by the standard of the fruit. On the other hand, it is easy to judge too lightly. That is why it is so important to allow God to speak his assurance (or conviction of further need) through a combination of means. These dual criteria of the Spirit's witness and the Spirit's fruit serve as a very reliable channel through which God can speak.

Perhaps the most practical approach to the issue of assurance is simply to focus on the moment by moment aspect of the holy life. That is, daily spend private time with God in prayer, daily read and meditate on scripture, and daily renew the commitment of love and obedience to God. In such a scenario, questions of assurance tend to resolve themselves as a natural and relaxed intimacy with God is enjoyed.

9. How does a person become entirely sanctified?

Like the issue of assurance, this too can vary from person to person. For some, the entrance into entire sanctification is much like the entrance into conversion. There is conviction by the Holy Spirit of further need in the spiritual life which leads the person to an attitude of repentance and humility before God. But for others, the experience is more like a joyful celebration of overwhelming love for God. Words like consecration and surrender are often used when speaking of how to be entirely sanctified. Such terms, however, can create problems because they lead people to seek a formula for an experience rather than seeking a deeper relationship and closer walk with God.

As with assurance, the best way to seek entire sanctification is simply to seek God. Walk in daily obedience. Nurture the relationship with God through daily prayer and scripture reading. Each day renew the commitment of love for and obedience to God in all regards. In faith and trust, ask God to compete his work of entire sanctification in his own time and way. And finally, remember that it is his work to perform, not ours.

Many well-meaning believers struggle over the issue of becoming entirely sanctified either because they think they have to imitate another person's experience or because they are trying to tell God how to sanctify them. In either case, such a person is well advised to focus more on loving and obeying God and less on what they want God to do for them.

It must also be said that many people struggle to experience entire sanctification because they are seeking the wrong experience. There is no hope of experiencing a pure heart and perfect love if the actual problem is an unwillingness to forsake ongoing acts of sin. The true quest for holiness begins with the question, "Is there currently any willful sin in my life that has not been confessed, repented, and abandoned?"

15

Conclusion

"Make me what Thou wilt"

JOHN WESLEY'S theology has been described as a theology of balance, a theology for people, and a theology of salvation.[1]

It is a *theology of balance* in at least three ways. First, there is balance between freedom and responsibility. Although Wesleyanism has certain theological distinctives, it also allows for a certain degree of theological flexibility. For example, there is no single Wesleyan position on eschatology (doctrine of last things) or mode of baptism. These beliefs are left to individual interpretation. Yet Wesleyans take very seriously their responsibility to proclaim and live authentic biblical Christianity. The doctrines of universal sin, prevenient grace, the atonement of Christ, the reality of personal salvation, and the intimacy of entire sanctification are non-negotiable points of Wesleyan doctrine that are held firmly without apology. The Wesleyan balance is freedom on the non-essentials; responsibility on the essentials.

Second, Wesley's theology also strikes a balance between the doctrinal and the practical. His sermons and writings were generally constructed on a solid biblical and theological foundation. However, the most visible part of the structure was practical. Wesleyanism is committed to that same concept of practical theology.

Third, Wesley was controversial because he did not fit any of the established categories. Christians of his day were generally identified as Roman Catholic or Reformed Protestant. Wesley was neither and both. This balance between opposing traditions remains a hallmark of Wesleyanism. Although Wesleyans consider themselves to be squarely within the mainstream of Protestant evangelicalism, that mainstream does not always view Wesleyans in the same way. For, in fact, Wesleyanism does hold some doctrinal posi-

---

[1]   Lovett Haynes Weems Jr., *The Gospel According to Wesley: A Summary of John Wesley's Message* (Nashville: Discipleship Resources, 1982) 51–54.

tions that differ from the generic expression of contemporary evangelicalism. For example, Wesleyan theology embraces a more Catholic view of human freedom and responsibility, while at the same time affirming the Reformed emphasis on the sovereignty of God. This position seems inconsistent to some. To Wesleyans it is the biblical balance.

Wesleyanism is a *theology for people* in that it seeks to address the real needs of people at the point where they live. This was certainly Wesley's approach. Although he could and did associate with people of high society; his heart, time, and energy were committed to those with the greatest need. From riding in the death carts of condemned convicts, to building schools and shelters for orphans, to preaching the Good News of Christ to coal miners at the entrance of the pits, he brought theology out of the church and university and took it to the people. Wesleyanism has always been a theology and a ministry for real people in the real world.

Above all else, Wesleyanism is a *theology of salvation*. Not salvation by works, nor salvation by arbitrary decree, but personal salvation by grace through faith in Christ. Every point of Wesleyan doctrine and every act of Wesleyan ministry is ultimately about bringing people to saving faith in Christ. It is about pointing them toward the transformation of new birth in him, the subsequent life of holiness here, and the life of eternal joy hereafter. The goal of Christian experience in the Wesleyan tradition is to see all people everywhere joining together in the prayer that John Wesley utilized in his *Covenant Service*:

> Lord Jesus, if Thou wilt receive me into Thy house, if Thou wilt but own me as Thy servant, I will not stand upon terms. Impose on me what condition Thou pleasest; write down Thy own articles; command me what Thou wilt; let me be Thy servant.
>
> Make me what Thou wilt; Lord, and set me where Thou wilt. Let me be a vessel of silver or gold, or a vessel of wood or stone; so I be a vessel of honor. I am content. If I be not the head, or the eye, or the ear, one of the nobler and more honorable instruments Thou wilt employ, let me be the hand, or the foot, as one of the lowest and least esteemed of all the servants of my Lord.
>
> Lord, put me to what Thou wilt; rank me with whom Thou wilt. Put me to doing; put me to suffering. Let me be employed for Thee, or laid aside for Thee, exalted for Thee, or trodden under foot for Thee. Let me be full; let me be empty. Let me have all things; let me have nothing.
>
> I freely and heartily resign all to Thy pleasure and disposal.[2]

---

[2] *Wesley Hymns*, compiled by Ken Bible (Kansas City: Lillenas, 1982) A7–A8.

Bibliography

Arminius, James. *The Writings of James Arminius*. Translated by James Nicholas and W. R. Bagnall. Grand Rapids: Baker, 1977.

Bennet, John. *Mirror of the Soul: The Diary of an Early Methodist Preacher, John Bennet: 1714–1754*. Edited by Simon Ross Valentine. Peterborough: Methodist Publishing, 2002.

Bassett, Paul M., and William M. Greathouse. *Exploring Christian Holiness*. Vol. 2: *The Historical Development*. Kansas City: Beacon Hill, 1985.

Bonhoeffer, Dietrich. *Ethics*. Edited by Eberhard Bethge New York: Macmillan, 1979.

Bosch, David J. *Transforming Mission: Paradigm Shifts in Theology of Mission*. Maryknoll, N.Y.: Orbis, 1998.

Butler, David. *Methodism and Papists: John Wesley and the Catholic Church in the Eighteenth Century*. London: Darton, Longman and Todd, 1995.

Calvin, John. *Calvin's Institutes*. Abridged ed. Edited by Donald K. McKim. Louisville: Westminster John Knox, 2001.

Collins, Kenneth J. "Twentieth Century Interpretations of John Wesley's Aldersgate Experience: Coherence or Confusion." *WTJ* 24 (1989) 18–31.

———. *The Scripture Way of Salvation: The Heart of John Wesley's Theology*. Nashville: Abingdon, 1997.

———. *A Real Christian: The Life of John Wesley*. Nashville: Abingdon, 1999.

———. *John Wesley: A Theological Journey*. Nashville: Abingdon, 2003.

Cox, Leo G. *John Wesley's Concept of Perfection*. Kansas City: Beacon Hill, 1964.

Dallimore, Arnold. *Susanna: The Mother of John and Charles Wesley*. Durham: Evangel, 1992.

Dayton, Wilber T. "Entire Sanctification: The Divine Purification and Perfection of Man." In *A Contemporary Wesleyan Theology: Biblical, Systematic, and Practical*, volume 1. Grand Rapids: Francis Asbury, 1983.

Drury, Keith W. *Holiness for Ordinary People*. Indianapolis: Wesleyan, 1993.

Dunning, H. Ray. *Grace, Faith, and Holiness: A Wesleyan Systematic Theology*. Kansas City: Beacon Hill, 1988.

Fletcher Joseph. *Situation Ethics: The New Morality*. Philadelphia: Westminster, 1966.

Foster, Richard J. *Celebration of Discipline: The Path to Spiritual Growth*. 20th Anniversary ed. New York: HarperCollins, 1998.

Grider, J. Kenneth. *Entire Sanctification: The Distinctive Doctrine of Wesleyanism*. Kansas City: Beacon Hill, 1980.

———. *A Wesleyan–Holiness Theology*. Kansas City: Beacon Hill, 1994.

Hattersley, Roy. *A Brand from the Burning: The Life of John Wesley*. London: Little Brown, 2002.

Heitzenrater, Richard P. *Wesley and the People Called Methodists*. Nashville: Abingdon, 1995.

Henderson, D. Michael. *John Wesley's Class Meeting: A Model for Making Disciples*. Nappanee, Ind.: Evangel, 1997.

Kent, John. *Wesley and the Wesleyans: Religion in Eighteenth-Century Britain*. Cambridge: Cambridge University Press, 2002.

Lewis, C. S. "Surprised by Joy." In *The Inspirational Writings of C. S. Lewis.* New York: Inspirational, 1994.

Lindström, Harald. *Wesley and Sanctification: A Study in the Doctrine of Salvation.* London: Epworth, 1950; Reprinted, Nappanne, Ind.: Francis Asbury, 1996.

Maddox, Randy L. "John Wesley—Practical Theologian?" *WTJ* 23 (1988) 122–47.

————. *Responsible Grace: John Wesley's Practical Theology.* Nashville: Kingswood, 1994.

McGrath, Alister E. *Christian Spirituality: An Introduction.* Oxford: Blackwell, 1999.

Noll, Mark A. *Turning Points: Decisive Moments in the History of Christianity.* Grand Rapids: Baker, 1997.

Oden, Thomas C. *John Wesley's Scriptural Christianity: A Plain Exposition of His Teachings on Christian Doctrine.* Grand Rapids: Zondervan, 1994.

Oswalt, John N. *Called to be Holy: A Biblical Perspective.* Nappanee, Ind.: Evangel, 1999.

Outler, Albert C. *John Wesley.* New York: Oxford University Press, 1964.

Purkiser, W. T. *Exploring Christian Holiness.* Vol. 1: *The Biblical Foundations.* Kansas City: Beacon Hill, 1983.

Rack, Henry D. *Reasonable Enthusiast: John Wesley and the Rise of Methodism.* London: Epworth, 1992.

Robinson, John A. T. *Christian Freedom in a Permissive Society.* Philadelphia: Westminster, 1970.

Runyon, Theodore. *The New Creation: John Wesley's Theology Today.* Nashville: Abingdon, 1998.

Staples, Rob L. *Outward Sign and Inward Grace: The Place of Sacraments in Wesleyan Spirituality.* Kansas City: Beacon Hill, 1991.

Stone, Ronald H. *John Wesley's Life and Ethics.* Nashville: Abingdon, 2001.

Tracy, Wesley D., E. Dee Freeborn, Janine Tartaglia, and Morris A. Weigelt. *The Upward Call: Spiritual Formation and the Holy Life.* Kansas City: Beacon Hill, 1994.

Turner, John Munsey. *John Wesley: The Evangelical Revival and the Rise of Methodism in England.* Peterborough: Epworth, 2002.

Volz, Carl A. *Faith and Practice in the Early Church: Foundations for Contemporary Theology.* Minneapolis: Augsburg, 1983.

Walsh, John. "Methodism and the Origins of English-Speaking Evangelicalism." In *Evangelicalism: Comparative Studies of Popular Protestantism in North America, the British Isles, and Beyond, 1700–1990,* edited by Mark A. Noll, David W. Bebbington, and George A. Rawlyk, 19–37. Oxford: Oxford University, 1994.

Ware, Timothy. *The Orthodox Church.* Rev. ed. London: Penguin, 1997.

Weems, Lovett Haynes, Jr. *The Gospel according to Wesley: A Summary of John Wesley's Message.* Nashville: Discipleship Resources, 1982.

Wesley, Charles, and John Wesley. *Wesley Hymns.* Compiled by Ken Bible. Kansas City: Lillenas, 1982.

Wesley, John. *Primitive Physick: or An Easy and Natural Method of Curing Most Diseases.* London: Trye, 1747.

————. *The Works of John Wesley.* 3d ed. Edited by Thomas Jackson. London: Wesleyan Methodist Book Room, 1872. Reprint, Kansas City: Beacon Hill, 1979.

————. *The Works of John Wesley.* Edited by Reginald W. Ward and Richard P. Heitzenrater. Bicentennial ed. Nashville: Abingdon, 1988.

———— . *John Wesley's Sermons: An Anthology.* Edited by Albert C. Outler and Richard P. Heitzenrater. Nashville: Abingdon, 1991.

Wiley, H. Orton. *Christian Theology.* 3 vols. Kansas City: Beacon Hill, 1940–43.

Wirt, Sherwood E. *The Confessions of Augustine in Modern English.* Grand Rapids: Zondervan, 1981.

Wood, A. Skevington. *The Burning Heart: John Wesley, Evangelist.* Grand Rapids: Eerdmans, 1967.

Yrigoyen, Charles Jr. *John Wesley: Holiness of Heart and Life.* New York: The Mission Education and Cultivation Program Department for the Women's Division, General Board of Global Ministries, The United Methodist Church, 1996.